SPORTS STARS WITH HEART
Albert Pujols
MVP ON AND OFF THE FIELD

by Tom Needham

Enslow Publishers, Inc.
40 Industrial Road
Box 398
Berkeley Heights, NJ 07922
USA
http://www.enslow.com

Library of Congress Cataloging-in-Publication Data
Needham, Tom.
  Albert Pujols : MVP on and off the field / by Tom Needham.
      p. cm. — (Sports stars with heart)
  Includes bibliographical references and index.
  ISBN-13: 978-0-7660-2866-1
  ISBN-10: 0-7660-2866-6
  1. Pujols, Albert, 1980—Juvenile literature. 2. Baseball players—
Dominican Republic—Biography—Juvenile literature. 3. St. Louis Cardinals
(Baseball team) I. Title.
  GV865.P85N44 2007
  796.357092—dc22
    [B]   2006031843

Credits
Editorial Direction: Red Line Editorial, Inc. (Bob Temple)
Editor: Sue Green
Design and Page Production: The Design Lab

Printed in the United States of America

10 9 8 7 6 5 4 3 2

To Our Readers: We have done our best to make sure all Internet
addresses in this book were active and appropriate when we went to press.
However, the author and the publisher have no control over and assume no
liability for the material available on those Internet sites or on other Web
sites they may link to. Any comments or suggestions can be sent by e-mail
to comments@enslow.com or to the address on the back cover.

Photographs © 2007: AP Photo/Elise Amendola: 109, 110; AP Photo/Al
Behrman: 55, 79, 89; AP Photo/Paul Connors: 70; AP Photo/Kyle Ericson: 7, 36;
AP Photo/James A. Finley: 3, 10, 18, 92; AP Photo/Lenny Ignelzi: 3, 27; AP
Photo/Tom Gannam: 1, 3, 47, 64, 74, 77; AP Photo/Eric Gay:81; AP Photo/Charlie
Neibergall: 99; AP Photo/David J. Phillip: 42, 83; AP Photo/Denis Poroy: 103; AP
Photo/Ed Reinke: 58; AP Photo/Jeff Roberson: 4; AP Photo/Ted S. Warren: 28

Cover Photo: Albert Pujols tips his cap to the fans after breaking the
National League rookie RBI record September 19, 2001. Pujols earned three
RBIs against the Milwaukee Brewers to bring his total to 120. The previous
record of 119 was set by Wally Berger of the Boston Braves in 1930.

C O N T E N T S

Albert Pujols bats against the Chicago Cubs in 2006.

1

A Star Is Discovered

When a special moment in sports is about to happen, fans can often sense it. When former New England Patriots kicker Adam Vinatieri lined up to kick Super Bowl-winning field goals twice, fans just knew the ball would sail through the uprights. When Michael Jordan released a shot to win a game for the Chicago Bulls, people expected it to find nothing but net. And when the St. Louis Cardinals need a big hit and Albert Pujols steps to the plate, it is a pretty good bet that the Cards' hard-hitting hero will come through.

TOP TEN HOME RUN HITTERS AS OF 2007 SEASON

1	Barry Bonds	762
2	Hank Aaron	755
3	Babe Ruth	714
4	Willie Mays	660
5	Sammy Sosa	609
6	Ken Griffey	593
7	Frank Robinson	586
8	Mark McGwire	583
9	Harmon Killebrew	573
10	Rafael Palmerio	569

ALBERT PUJOLS FILE

Full name: Jose Albert Pujols
Birthplace: Santo Domingo, Dominican Republic
Height: 6' 3"
Weight: 225 pounds
Date of birth: January 16, 1980
Bats: Right
Throws: Right
College: Maple Woods Community College in Missouri
Position: First baseman
MLB team: St. Louis Cardinals
MLB debut: April 2, 2001
Acquired: Thirteenth round, 1999

Such was the case on April 29, 2006, when St. Louis hosted the Washington Nationals. With the game tied at one heading into the bottom of the eighth inning, Pujols trotted out to the plate. St. Louis' beloved power hitter had already belted 13 home runs during the first month of the season, tying the all-time April record held by Ken Griffey Jr. (1997) and Luis Gonzalez (2001).

Pujols, arguably the best player in the game today, has always been more interested in winning than compiling statistics. His team needed him. All he wanted was to see the right pitch.

Pujols worked the count to 2–1 off Washington pitcher Jon Rauch. On the next

Pujols swings for a home run against the Washington Nationals April 29, 2006, at Busch Stadium in St. Louis.

pitch, Rauch tried the outside of the plate. The right-handed Pujols was ready. The sound of the bat connecting with the ball echoed through Busch Stadium as cameras flashed. The ball kept traveling and traveling until it finally landed 411 feet away in the Cardinals' right-field bullpen.

It was home run number 14.

Pujols' solo shot put the Cardinals on top for an eventual 2–1 victory and made him the record holder for the most home runs ever hit in the month of April.

"It's always a thrill to see history," St. Louis manager Tony La Russa said. "But to see it in a game situation like that adds a little more to the story we're all going to tell some time."[1]

That home run concluded yet another chapter in Pujols' story. It is a story about a player who believed in himself when others did not. When critics said he could not do it, Pujols knew he could. He has become the most feared hitter in Major League Baseball (MLB). He was the first player in major-league history to hit thirty or more home runs in each of his first five seasons. He also was the first to collect 100 RBIs in each of his first five seasons since Ted Williams did it in the 1940s.

Pujols is a team player, a family man, and well on his way to a Hall of Fame career. He is everything that is right about baseball and is humbled by his own extraordinary talent.

His story is one of pride, perseverance, and humble beginnings. At the core of his story is a man with a childlike love for baseball who also loves life. Today, he is widely recognized as the one of the game's best players—perhaps, the best. There was a time, however, when he was considered nothing more than a long shot to make a roster.

MAKING A NAME FOR HIMSELF

In 2001, Pujols, at the age of twenty-one, arrived in Jupiter, Florida, for Cardinals spring training. The chances of him making the team seemed remote. Most of the attention was focused on Mark McGwire, who entered the season 46 home runs shy of becoming the fourth player in league history with 600 home runs. Big things were expected from the team, as well, with a roster that included stars such as McGwire, Jim Edmonds, J.D. Drew, and Bobby Bonilla. There were few roster spots available.

BIG MAC ATTACK

Albert Pujols' first season in 2001 was the last season for legendary St. Louis power hitter Mark McGwire. "Big Mac" played Major League Baseball from 1986 to 2001 and with the Cardinals from 1997 to 2001. In 1998, McGwire broke Roger Maris' single-season home run record (61) with 70. The record was broken in 2001 by Barry Bonds (73). McGwire finished his career with 583 home runs, ranking fifth at the time.

Pujols had made a name for himself in the organization with a meteoric rise through the minor leagues. A thirteenth-round draft pick in 1999, Pujols opened 2000 with Class-A Peoria. He battered opposing pitchers on the way to being named Most Valuable

Pujols and his wife, Deidre, arrive at a news conference November 12, 2001, after he was named National League Rookie of the Year.

Player (MVP) of the Midwest League. Later in the year, he was assigned to Triple-A Memphis and helped the Redbirds advance to the Triple-A World Series.

Pujols was named MVP of the Pacific Coast League playoffs after batting .367 with 2 home runs and 5 RBIs in seven playoff games. It had been quite a ride for Pujols, who was named the organization's Minor League Player of the Year.

Earning a spot in the big leagues, however, still seemed like a stretch. The Cardinals' trade of third baseman and budding star Fernando Tatis in the off-season to the Montreal Expos showed, however, that the Cardinals were aware of what Pujols might one day become.

ST. LOUIS CARDINALS' MINOR-LEAGUE AFFILIATIONS
AAA: Memphis Redbirds, Pacific Coast League
AA: Springfield Cardinals, Texas League
Advanced A: Palm Beach Cardinals, Florida State League
A: Swing of the Quad Cities, Midwest League
Short A: State College Spikes, New York-Penn League
Rookie: Johnson City Cardinals, Appalachian League

With Tatis out of the picture, the likely third-base platoon for the Cardinals was a combination of veteran infielders Placido Polanco, Craig Paquette, and Shane Andrews. An already crowded outfield also made it unlikely that Pujols could crack the roster there. Newly acquired Bonilla and journeyman John Mabry seemed to have inside tracks to the final roster spots, and it was almost certain that Pujols was destined for a return to Triple-A Memphis to start the season.

DETERMINATION AND DESIRE

As the spring progressed, Pujols did all he could to show the Cardinals that he was a versatile player worthy of a roster spot. He played several different positions and put up solid numbers—batting .306 with 3 home runs and 10 RBIs. He kept working hard, kept doing whatever was asked of him, and kept his faith.

On the final weekend of the spring exhibition schedule, Pujols found himself in a battle with Mabry and Bernard Gilkey for the final roster spot. On March 31, 2001, the announcement Pujols had waited a lifetime to hear was made: The team purchased his contract. Pujols was officially a Major League Baseball player.

REWRITING HISTORY

It is commonly thought that a hamstring injury to Bobby Bonilla opened the door for Albert Pujols to make the opening-day, twenty-five-man St. Louis Cardinals roster in 2001. While it is true that Bonilla was placed on the fifteen-day disabled list to start the season and Pujols' power and versatility helped fill the void, Bonilla's injury actually paved the way for outfielder John Mabry to make the team.

Pujols' contract was purchased on March 31, 2001. Mabry's contract was purchased the following day, filling the final roster spot and signifying that Pujols had made the team regardless of Bonilla's health. On April 9, Bonilla was activated, and Mabry was sent to the Florida Marlins for cash considerations.

General manager Walt Jocketty said that bringing Pujols to St. Louis with the team felt like the right thing to do. "He's unproven, but he's certainly shown every indication he can compete at the major-league level," Jocketty said. "We'll see what develops."[2]

Something developed, all right. Something very special developed.

CHAPTER TWO

A Boy and His Dreams

Jose Alberto Pujols was born on January 16, 1980, in Santo Domingo in the Dominican Republic. Life was not easy for the Pujols family. They did not live in a traditional house with the comforts that most American families do. In fact, by most accounts, they were poor and relied on government-assistance programs.

Albert's father, Bienvenido, was not around much during his son's youth. Albert received most of his parental care from his grandmother, America. She was the driving force in his upbringing and stressed values, hard work, and compassion. She made sure Albert did the right things and learned the lessons necessary to become a good person. Ten uncles and aunts were

HOME SWEET HOME

Santo Domingo is the capital of the Dominican Republic, an island nation. The city is located in the southern part of the island. It has an estimated population of 2.2 million people. The city was founded in 1498 by Bartholomew Columbus, brother of Christopher Columbus.

also big parts of Albert's upbringing. He looked upon them as brothers and sisters. America kept the family unit together.

Though the Pujols family did not have much money or material goods, they did not know any other lifestyle. They did know, however, that they could rely on one another. Their love for one another helped them through the tough times, and America instilled a strong belief and love for God in the family.

"What motivated me more than money are God and my family," said Albert.[1]

Albert still lives by those principles today.

A FIELD OF DREAMS

Albert's love for baseball began at an early age. By the time he was six years old, he knew he wanted to become a professional baseball player. His father was well-known in the Dominican Republic as an outstanding pitcher. That made Albert very proud, and he spent many of his childhood days playing baseball on the fields near his home. Using a stick for a bat, a milk carton for a glove, and a lime as a ball, he did his best to develop his skills. America taught him to appreciate the things he had.

He remembers those days well. He worked at the game he loved whenever he had the chance on the tattered fields in his neighborhood.

"Average fields, not as good as here in the States," recalled Albert. "No walls. A lot of ground-ball home runs."[2]

A HOTBED FOR BASEBALL TALENT

Baseball is far and away the most popular sport in the Dominican Republic, and the country has produced many Major League Baseball stars. In fact, there have been 410 MLB players from the island between 1956 and 2005. The approximate number of Dominican Republic-born players currently signed to MLB organizations (including minor leagues) is 1,521. The star-studded list of players from Albert Pujols' hometown of Santo Domingo includes Manny Ramirez, David Ortiz, Aramis Ramirez, and Placido Polanco.

Albert did not have a favorite baseball team, but he loved the game. He showed surprising ability at an early age. When he stepped to the plate, he often imagined he was Dominican-born star Julio Franco. In fact, he modeled his batting stance after Franco's. He admired how Franco held the bat high and used a wide stance to jump on pitches.

"I was flattered when I first heard that Albert pictured my swing as the one he wanted to use," said

Franco, a three-time MLB all-star. "We've talked a lot about how you have to be aggressive and make yourself a tough out."[3]

Franco admits that Albert learned to take hitting to a level he never reached. "I could never be confused with having the power he has," Franco said.[4]

Albert learned a great deal about hitting by imitating Franco. He improved his technique and developed the right mindset to become a consistent hitter. He also recognized how important it was to attack pitches. "You can't be passive at the plate," Albert said. "You have to be in control."[5]

Since money was always scarce for the Pujols family, Albert did not have the chance to go to fancy baseball camps or receive individual

JULIO FRANCO FILE

Full name: Julio César Robles Franco

Birthplace: San Pedro de Macoris, Dominican Republic

Height: 6' 1"

Weight: 210 pounds

Date of birth: August 23, 1958

Bats: Right

Throws: Right

Position: First baseman

MLB team: New York Mets

MLB debut: April 23, 1982 (Philadelphia Phillies)

Notes: A three-time all-star, Franco has a career batting average of .298 and is the all-time hits leader among Dominican-born players. At forty-eight, he is famous for being the oldest regular-position player in major-league history.

training. Whatever money the family had went toward providing the bare necessities.

"I never lifted weights as a kid," said Albert. "I couldn't get really strong because there wasn't enough to eat in a big family like mine."[6]

The Pujols family made the best of what they had. And Albert never wavered in believing in his dream of one day reaching the big leagues. Watching the success of Dominican players such as Franco only fueled Albert's desires more.

THE LAND OF OPPORTUNITY

Searching for a better quality of life, the Pujols family migrated to the United States. When Albert was sixteen, he moved to New York City with his father. But New York City was not what they expected. In fact, Albert actually witnessed a man being shot one day. America stepped in and demanded safer surroundings for her family.

WHERE'S INDEPENDENCE?

Independence, the city Albert Pujols moved to after living in New York City, is located in Missouri and was founded in 1827. It is in the Kansas City metropolitan area and has an approximate population of 113,288 people. President Harry S. Truman spent his childhood in Independence. Truman, the thirty-third president of the United States, held office from 1945 to 1953.

Pujols points upward after hitting a home run.

So, the family was on the move again. They packed up their belongings and headed for the Midwest. They made Independence, Missouri, their new home. With a grandmother named America to guide him and a city called Independence to live in, what could be better for young Albert?

Once in Independence, Albert enrolled as a student at Fort Osage High School. It was not an easy transition for him. Not only was he the new kid, he also had a bit of a language barrier. Naturally a Spanish speaker, Albert did not know English well. However, he did his best to fit in.

In the beginning, making friends was not easy. He did not know anybody. At times he felt like a stranger in a strange land. "[There were] no Dominicans, besides me and my cousins," he said.[7]

On the baseball field, however, Albert did not have to speak. His bat did the speaking for him.

Fort Osage baseball coach Dave Fry recalled the first day Albert walked into his science class. Through a cousin who served as an interpreter, Albert announced, "I want to play baseball."

"The baseball gods were smiling on me that day," said Fry.[8]

"The baseball gods were smiling on me that day."

—Dave Fry

CHAPTER THREE

Building a Resume

Fort Osage High School had never seen the likes of Albert Pujols. He entered the school as a sophomore, and while his English was not yet as good as that of his classmates, his skills on the baseball field were far more advanced than any of his teammates.

One of the images that comes to Fort Osage coach David Fry's mind when he thinks about his days coaching Albert is a memorable hit during a game at Liberty High School. Albert uncorked a mammoth shot that seemed as if it would never land. It eventually did—about four hundred fifty feet (one hundred thirty-seven meters) from home plate and on top of a twenty-five-foot-high air-conditioning unit.

Albert was a coach's dream. He worked hard in the classroom, and he stayed out of trouble. Many young athletes with special talents take their skills for granted. But Albert always strived to be better. Helping Fort Osage win was a priority for Albert, but he also knew that if he really wanted to attain his goal of reaching the major leagues, he needed to continually get better.

"He was so driven to succeed, always stayed behind to take extra batting practice or ground balls," said Fry.[1]

Albert, who proudly wore his uniform to school on game days, hit 11 home runs and had a batting average higher than .500 in his first season at Fort Osage. He earned All-State honors while the team captured the state championship with a 21–7 record.

His reputation began to grow. The following season, opposing teams often chose to simply pitch around him. In 88 at-bats, he drew 55

> **"He was so driven to succeed, always stayed behind to take extra batting practice or ground balls."**
>
> **—Dave Fry**

"**I knew Albert had the talent to make it into pro ball. He had a really good feel about the pitch coming in. He would take a lot of walks for us but when he got the pitch he liked, he hit it hard every time.**"

—Dave Fry

walks. That meant that Albert reached base 62 percent of the time without even having to hit the ball.

Despite rarely seeing pitches he could hit, Albert hit 8 home runs and earned All-State honors for the second time.

"I knew Albert had the talent to make it into pro ball," said Fry. "He had a really good feel about the pitch coming in. He would take a lot of walks for us but when he got the pitch he liked, he hit it hard every time."[2]

Albert had certainly caught the eye of several MLB scouts. Listening to their advice, he decided his best option would be to accelerate his classroom workload and graduate early. Albert studied extra hard in the fall and had enough credits to graduate in January. It meant forgoing his senior year of baseball, but he could make the move to the next level more quickly, with his ultimate goal of reaching the bigs squarely in his sights.

GIVING IT THE COLLEGE TRY

While studying to graduate from high school early, Albert participated in a high school all-star game in the Kansas City area. Maple Wood Community College baseball coach Marty Kilgore attended the game. Kilgore was so impressed with Albert that he recruited him to the nearby school for the spring of 1999.

Albert was an immediate success. In his first game, he blasted a grand slam home run and turned a rare unassisted triple play while playing shortstop. He did not stop there. Albert put on a show all season long. He finished the campaign with 22 home runs and 80 RBIs. He batted .461. At this point, it was clear he had developed into a serious prospect.

Despite speculation that Albert could be drafted as high as the fifth round, rumors arose that he was not in shape and did not have a natural position. Some also questioned his age. Since Albert was not born in the United States, the facts of his birth date were not easy to find.

When draft day finally came, it was a letdown. Albert was not drafted until the thirteenth round by the St. Louis Cardinals.

OOPS—MAKE THAT 401 OOPS

Had Major League clubs known then what they know now, it is hard to imagine any player being chosen ahead of Albert Pujols in the 1999 MLB draft. The reality is, however, that there were 401 players selected ahead of him.

Missing out on Albert stings the Kansas City Royals perhaps most of all since Albert's high school, Fort Osage High School, is located only about twenty miles (thirty-two kilometers) away from the Royals' Kauffman Stadium. Russ Meyer, a Kansas City businessman who had a brief stint with the Royals' farm system, can only shake his head now about what might have been. He saw Albert's skills firsthand. Meyer coached Albert in a summer baseball league.

"I was doing some bird-dogging for the Royals at the time, and in my report I wrote that I thought (Pujols) had the potential to be drafted in the third to fifth round," said Meyer. "Turns out that I underestimated him, too."

"Here's the kicker," said Herk Robinson, who was the Royals' general manager at the time. "We had someone in our engineering department here at Kauffman Stadium who actually lived with Albert for about three months. You can't get much more in your backyard than that."

Of course, the Royals were not the only team to overlook Albert. In fact, among MLB front offices, Albert is regarded as the big one who got away.

Jay Darnell was a scout with the Colorado Rockies at the time. He said, "I remember pulling into a truck stop and leaving a voice mail. I told them, 'Just in case something happens, I think this guy (Pujols) is going to hit for a lot of power.'"

Fortunately for the Cardinals, Darnell's recommendation was not taken.

Dan Jennings, vice president of player development and scouting for the Florida Marlins, was the scouting director for the Tampa Bay Devil Rays in 1999. One of his scouts could not stop talking about some hot prospect at a junior college in Kansas City. Jennings still regrets not listening to his scout.

"That was obviously the biggest mistake we made when I was in Tampa Bay," said Jennings. "If we had picked him in the ninth round, we'd look like geniuses."

Few people looked like geniuses in regard to Albert Pujols and the 1999 MLB Draft—except, of course, for the team that decided the 402nd pick was worth the gamble.

He was offered $10,000 to sign with the club, but thought he could do better. So, he passed on the offer and decided to play that summer in the Jayhawk League, a circuit for college-age players based in western Kansas.

"That was very frustrating," said Kilgore. "I tried to tell [Albert] that a lot of the scouts in the Midwest didn't know what they were doing."[3]

The Jayhawk League prohibited the use of aluminum bats, but that was no problem for Albert. He was used to swinging wooden bats and led his team, the Hays Larks, in batting average and home runs.

At the end of the summer, the Cardinals decided to increase their offer to $60,000. This time, Pujols chose to accept it.

TO SIGN OR NOT TO SIGN?

The Major League Baseball draft is a complicated process, complete with various scenarios that make a player eligible or ineligible. In its most basic form, eligible players are:

• High school players, if they have graduated and have not yet attended college.

• Four-year college players who have completed at least their junior season and are at least twenty-one years old.

• Junior college players.

• Twenty-one-year-old players.

If a team selects a player, it retains his rights until one week prior to the next draft or until the player becomes ineligible based on the previous criteria. During that time, the team may negotiate with the player. If the player chooses not to sign with the team that selected him, he may re-enter the draft in the future.

Pujols watches his two-run home run against the Arizona Diamondbacks in Game 2 of the 2001 National League Division Series.

A MINOR STOP

Dave Karaff, the regional scout who signed Pujols, now reflects back on the organization's original question about the future star. Today that question seems almost silly.

Pujols walks back to the Cardinals' dugout after hitting a home run against the Cincinnati Reds August 23, 2001.

"My one fear was whether he was going to hit, if you can believe that," Karaff says with a laugh. "If we all felt he could hit consistently, he would have been a first-rounder and got his $3 million bonus.

"He still does some of the things that I feared, but he has the ability to make adjustments, and that's something I never saw. He was a power guy, he had great hands, great arm. I felt he could play third base."[4]

Despite all the money and resources that major-league clubs use to analyze prospects, some good ones always slip through the cracks. St. Louis was truly fortunate to be able to get a player like Pujols with a thirteenth-round draft choice.

"The Cardinals were lucky," Karaff said. "The other clubs, I don't know what they were thinking. People asked, 'Where was he going to play?' People talked about him as a catcher. Hindsight is great. You can ask any scout . . . I know of one club, maybe two, where the area scout had him rated up there, but he went for a workout and didn't perform well."[5]

No matter what Karaff's concerns might have been about Pujols, those fears are now a distant memory. Now, says the former Cardinals scout, he is just glad he had the chance to be a part of bringing him on board.

"I'm proud of the fact that I have an association with him," said Karaff. "What makes me feel best is he's a great kid. After he got to the big leagues, we had meetings in St. Louis, and I asked him what his first thought was when he walked in there. He said, 'Dave, I knew I'd be here.'"[6]

Pujols' stay in the minors was brief. He dominated every level he was assigned to and scooped up many awards. When he finished his first season of minor-league play, he joined the Arizona Fall League and honed his skills at third base while batting .323.

The Cardinals had seen enough of their budding star to invite him to spring training in 2001. The plan was for the club to get a good look at how Pujols

ELITE COMPANY

In 2004, Albert Pujols was named to the Arizona Fall League (AFL) Hall of Fame. Pujols played for the 2000 Scottsdale Scorpions. The AFL, created in 1992, is owned and operated by Major League Baseball and serves as a finishing school for top prospects. More than one thousand players who came through the league have reached the majors. To qualify for the honor, a player must have achieved recognition on the major-league level as a Rookie of the Year, MVP, All-Star MVP, Gold Glove winner, or Silver Slugger award recipient. There are seventeen AFL members in the hall.

ARIZONA FALL LEAGUE HALL OF FAMERS

Garret Anderson	Grady Little
Dusty Baker	Jerry Manuel
Terry Francona	Tony Peña
Nomar Garciaparra	Troy Percival
Jason Giambi	Mike Piazza
Shawn Green	Albert Pujols
Roy Halladay	Mike Scioscia
Todd Helton	Alfonso Soriano
Derek Jeter	

would fare against major-league competition and then likely send him back to Triple-A Memphis. Pujols, however, had other plans.

> ## "I am going there to make the team."
>
> **—Albert Pujols**

"I was kidding him about how neat it was going to be, throwing to Mark McGwire during infield (practice)," said Kilgore. "I mean, no one expected Albert to be on the team right away. But Albert looked at me— dead serious—and just said, 'I am not going there to throw to Mark McGwire. I am going there to make the team.'"[7]

CHAPTER FOUR

Falling in Love

During his journey through the minor leagues, Albert Pujols did not have a lot of time for many things other than baseball. But he stepped out of character one evening and decided to go to a dance club in Kansas City. It turned out to be an evening that would change the course of his life forever.

While at the club, a young lady caught his eye. This young lady, named Deidre Corona, was also interested in Pujols. The two started talking and hit it off. Pujols decided he would take a chance and asked Deidre to go on a date with him. She accepted. Their first date was a dinner at the Cheesecake Factory. It was there that both Pujols and Deidre came clean about some information they did not share at the dance club.

"He told me that he had lied about his age," Deidre said. "He told me he was 21, but he was only 18."[1]

Lying was not in Pujols' nature. However, he had done it because he did not think Deidre, who was twenty-one, would go on the date if she knew what his true age was. As it turned out, he was not the only one being less than honest.

"I had a confession of my own," Deidre said.[2]

Deidre explained to Pujols that she was a single mother. She had an infant daughter. And there was more. Her daughter, Isabella, suffered from Down syndrome, an incurable disease that often includes a combination of birth defects.

> **WHAT IS DOWN SYNDROME?**
> One of the most common genetic birth defects, Down syndrome affects approximately one in eight hundred to one thousand babies. The incurable disorder includes a combination of birth defects. Among them can be some degree of mental retardation, heart defects, problems with vision and hearing, and other health issues. The severity of the disease varies greatly among those affected by it. It is generally caused by an extra chromosome and is named after John Langdon Down, the British doctor who first described it in 1866.

Deidre knew she was dropping a bombshell on Pujols. She was not sure if she would ever see him again after that evening. After all, most eighteen-year-olds with bright futures in baseball ahead of them would see this news as a problem they might not wish to tackle. But Deidre underestimated Pujols.

Pujols did not view Isabella and her affliction as a barrier. He liked Deidre, and he intended to see if their relationship would grow. Thrilled that Pujols wanted to continue their relationship, Deidre found some literature about Down syndrome written in Spanish and gave it to Pujols so he could fully understand. When Pujols met Isabella, he did not see a beautiful child with a terrible disease. He just saw a beautiful child.

"From the first moment they saw each other, Pujols and Isabella have had a special connection," Deidre said. "He loves to catch her eye, to make her smile."[3]

RIGHT TIME, RIGHT MOMENT

Pujols and Deidre's first meeting was like a tale in a storybook, complete with Deidre playing the role of damsel in distress and Pujols playing the knight. They overlooked each other's fibs and fell in love. There were issues to tackle, but despite their young ages, they maturely accepted the challenges. Deidre is convinced that meeting Pujols at that club was no accident.

"Albert never went to clubs," she said. "He did not drink. He didn't even want people smoking around him. He wasn't even old enough to be in the place. It was meant to be."[4]

Now, Deidre can only imagine what might have become of her and her child if she had not met Pujols that night in Kansas City. Isabella's father was not a part of their lives, and Deidre had been running with the wrong crowd. "I was broke," she said. "I lived at home. I had nothing."[5]

A FAMILY OF FAITH

The members of the Pujols family are dedicated Christians. Pujols credits his wife, Deidre, with pointing him in the right direction spiritually. She had been a Christian for several years before she met Pujols, and she brought him to a Bible study in the early stages of their relationship. Now, their faith is at the heart of their marriage.

"They are the real deal," said Missouri Baptist pastor Phil Hunter, who has performed many services with the Pujols family in attendance. "Sometimes when I am with Albert, I tell him to show the others his favorite position. He starts to get in a batting stance. That's when I stop him and remind him about what he does with Deidre when they both get down on their knees every night. That's when he drops down on his knees in a position of prayer.

"Every time that I see Albert, I ask him if he is still on his knees."

Many athletes thank God after a good performance on the field, but Hunter knows it is genuine with Pujols.

"Albert would have been a great baseball player—whether he was a Christian or not—because God graced him with the abilities," said Hunter. "But what Albert understands now is that it's not about him. It is about the Lord. Albert uses his platform (sports stardom) to share Christ with others."

Pujols holds the sign indicating only five games remained at Busch Stadium.

BACKYARD BASEBALL

Albert Pujols appears on the cover of *Backyard Baseball 2007*, a video game that transforms major-league players into kids playing in a sandlot setting. Pujols also serves as the acting spokesman for the game. He learned of the game by playing it with his son, A.J.

"My wife, Deidre, bought the game for my son, A.J., and he's loved it ever since," said Pujols. "So when we had the opportunity to become a part of it, I couldn't say no."

Pujols does not have much time to play video games but said *Backyard Baseball* is not only a fun game for children, it can be educational, as well.

"A video game like *Backyard Baseball* actually teaches kids the rules of baseball so they understand the game better when they watch it on TV or play with friends," he said. "It also helps kids understand real baseball strategies like when is the right time to steal, what pitches to hit, or when to try for a double play."

BUILDING A LIFE TOGETHER

Pujols and Deidre were married on New Year's Day of 2000. Shortly after, Pujols was assigned to the Cardinals' minor-league team in Peoria, Illinois. The future was looking bright, but the present was a struggle.

"Albert was making $252 every two weeks," said Deidre. "We were truly living on love! We ate a lot of mac 'n cheese in those days."[6]

While in Peoria, Deidre did all she could to find ways to make ends meet—and take care of Isabella—while Pujols did all he could to climb the ladder in the Cardinals' organization.

> **"Albert was making $252 every two weeks. We were truly living on love! We ate a lot of mac 'n cheese in those days."**
>
> **—Deidre Pujols**

"I did whatever it took," said Deidre. "I never just sat around hoping for the money angel to drop out of the sky. I sold Mary Kay [cosmetics] to be with Pujols and had to find places in Peoria that could assist Bella with her special needs."[7]

Today, of course, money is not an issue for the Pujols family, but they can always look back to the days when they had to "tough it out" as days filled with love and hope. In addition to Isabella, they now have a son, A.J., and another daughter, Sophia.

It takes a special kind of person to raise a special-needs child. Pujols and Deidre are that kind of people. In fact, in 2005, they launched the Pujols Family Foundation, which is dedicated to the love, care, and

> ## "We didn't choose Down syndrome. Down syndrome chose my family."
>
> **—Albert Pujols**

development of people with Down syndrome and their families.

Pujols and Deidre love all their children, and Pujols always finds time to make sure Isabella's needs are met. When the family gathers for meals, Pujols always make sure Isabella's place is set and her juice is waiting for her. And there are few things in the world he loves more than making funny faces for her, which always result in her giggling with excitement and love.

"We didn't choose Down syndrome," said Pujols. "Down syndrome chose my family."[8]

Like any good storybook, this fairy tale has a happy ending.

CHAPTER FIVE

5
Who Is That Rookie?

When opening day of the 2001 season rolled around, Albert Pujols found himself in a position that few—other than him—envisioned. He was an opening-day starter.

Pujols' major-league career began with him in left field playing against the Rockies in Colorado. He batted 3 times and got one hit. It was a start. The next series was a trip to Arizona where Pujols hit his first career home run. He finished the three-game series with 3 doubles and 8 RBIs. Pujols' fast start left the Cardinals with no choice but to leave him in the lineup.

Pujols slugs a 2-run homer against the Giants.

Meanwhile, in St. Louis, fans were beginning to wonder who this new person driving balls around the ballpark was. Pujols' debut at Busch Stadium was certainly memorable. He blasted a 2-run homer off Colorado pitcher Denny Neagle.

Pujols reached base 16 times in his first 34 plate appearances. He looked like a seasoned veteran, not a starry-eyed, twenty-one-year-old rookie. Pujols kept hitting, and by May 1, he had smashed 8 home runs, tying the rookie record held by Kent Hrbek and Carlos Delgado. For the month of April, Pujols batted .370 with 24 RBIs and was named the National League Rookie of the Month.

It was clear the Cardinals had made the right choice in keeping Pujols on the roster. And it was official: The St. Louis fans' love fest with Pujols had begun.

NO ORDINARY ROOKIE

Albert Pujols' fantastic rookie season was unmatched by anyone who had ever played for the St. Louis Cardinals before him. He became just the fourth rookie in major-league history, and the first in the National League, to hit at least .300 with 30 home runs, 100 RBIs, and 100 runs scored.

Albert Pujols' team rookie records

Home runs	37
Doubles	47
RBIs	130
Extra-base hits	88
Run scored	112
Total bases	360

"He is the whole package as far as a player," said manager Tony La Russa. "He commits to defense just like he does offense. He has natural talent. He's a young guy, very smart, very tough-minded."[1]

Fans wondered if the hot streak to start the season was nothing more than that, a streak. Could he really continue the pace? Many critics expected Pujols to cool down. He proved them wrong.

Pujols belted 8 more home runs in May to earn National League Rookie of the Month honors for the second straight month. His batting average ballooned to .353, and all any baseball fan in St. Louis could talk about was the new star.

HEY NOW, YOU'RE AN ALL-STAR

Pujols was clearly having an all-star season, perhaps even an MVP season. But there was one problem in regard to the All-Star Game. Pujols was not even listed on the ballots. Just like a bench player, his name was nowhere to be found.

Pujols' power and all-around play could not be denied, however. New York Mets manager Bobby Valentine, who coached the NL All-Stars in 2001, named Pujols to the team.

The American League won the game 4–1, thanks in part to an emotional third-inning home run by game MVP Cal Ripken Jr., who played in his eighteenth and final All-Star Game. Pujols did not see

CAL RIPKEN JR. FILE

Full name: Calvin Edwin Ripken Jr.

Birthplace: Havre de Grace, Maryland

Height: 6' 4"

Weight: 220 pounds

Date of birth: August 24, 1960

Bats: Right

Throws: Right

Positions: Shortstop, third baseman

MLB team: Baltimore Orioles
(retired 2001)

MLB debut: August 10, 1981

Acquired: Second round, 1978

NOTES: Known as baseball's "Iron Man," Cal Ripken Jr. snapped Lou Gehrig's consecutive games played record of 2,131 by playing in 2,632 games. Ripken played his entire twenty-one-year career with the Baltimore Orioles and was named an all-star nineteen times. A member of the 3,000-hit club, Ripken finished his career with 3,184 hits and 431 home runs while winning the Gold Glove award twice.

much action. He entered the game, held at Seattle's Safeco Field, in the eighth inning and played second base. In his only appearance at the plate, he drew a walk from Seattle pitcher Jeff Nelson.

Certainly Pujols would have liked to have had a chance to play more and show the baseball world what he could do on such a grand stage. In just four short months, however, Pujols had risen from a longshot for a roster spot to an all-star. He became the first Cardinals rookie to earn a trip to the Midsummer Classic since pitcher Luis Arroyo in 1955.

Pujols watches his double against Cincinnati August 15, 2001. The double extended Pujols' hitting streak to 16 games.

RUN TO THE PLAYOFFS

Pujols continued to amaze during the second half of the season. On August 4, he hit his twenty-sixth home run, a towering shot that went 453 feet. It was the longest home run by a Cardinal at Busch Stadium for the whole year. A few weeks later, he sent another rocket shot 439 feet over Cinergy Field's "Black Monster" center-field wall in Cincinnati.

Not only was Pujols playing amazing baseball, the Cardinals were winning. When the regular season ended, St. Louis finished in a tie with the Houston Astros with identical 93–69 records. The Astros won the tiebreaker format to become NL Central champions. The Cardinals won a Wild Card berth in the playoffs.

TOO BIG FOR LITTLE LEAGUE

The 2001 baseball season will always be remembered for the Little League fiasco involving the Rolando Paulino All-Stars of the Bronx, New York. The nation was fascinated with left-handed pitcher Danny Almonte and his incredible fastball. Almonte led his team to the Little League World Series and struck out 15 batters on the way to a perfect game in the World Series opener against Apopka, Florida.

The Bronx team finished third in the World Series, but documents surfaced proving Almonte was actually fourteen years old—too old to play. As a result, the team had to forfeit all of its wins. All records set by Almonte and the team were removed from the record book.

No one blamed Almonte, who apparently did not know the truth about his own age. The fault was with the adults who had allowed the incident to happen.

"Clearly, adults have used Danny Almonte and his teammates in a most contemptible and despicable way," said Little League president and CEO Stephen D. Keener. "We're clearly sad and angry that we were deceived. In fact, millions of Little Leaguers around the world were deceived."

St. Louis drew the eventual World Series champion Arizona Diamondbacks in the National League Division Series. The Cardinals played well, extending the best-of-five series to a winner-take-all fifth game, but they lost 2–1 when Tony Womack hit a two-out RBI single in the bottom of the ninth.

Pujols had a rough series, batting just .111 (2-for-18). His best moment came in Game 2 when he hit a 2-run, opposite-field homer off Randy Johnson in a 4–1 win.

The difference in the series was outstanding pitching by Arizona. Curt Schilling, who also won Game 1, struck out 9 Cardinals in the decisive game. For the series, St. Louis was only 2-for-33 with runners in scoring position.

"Believe me, it was a bitter defeat for our club. We really felt we were going to move forward," La Russa said. "But to be sitting on the bench and watching Curt Schilling and [Cardinals pitcher] Matt Morris, that isn't major league, that's a league above this one. It's really a privilege. When a guy does that kind of job, the loss is easier to take. I was thrilled to watch those two guys."[2]

WHAT A SEASON

While the season did not end the way Pujols would have liked, he was nothing short of spectacular. He played a team-high 161 games and led the team with a .329 batting average. He had 194 hits with 37 home runs, 47 doubles, and 130 RBIs. He also scored 112 runs.

He became the first Cardinal to lead his team in batting, home runs, RBIs, and runs scored since Ken Boyer did it in 1961. He also became the first Cardinal to win the team's Triple Crown since Ted Simmons in 1973.

Almost everything Pujols did in 2001 resulted in a Cardinals' rookie record, and he was named the National League Rookie of the Year. His play was so impressive that he finished fourth in the voting for the National League MVP award, which is selected by the Baseball Writers' Association of America. The winner was an easy choice as San Francisco's Barry Bonds set the all-time single-season home run record with 73.

2001 NATIONAL LEAGUE MVP VOTES

Voting for the 2001 National League Most Valuable Player award, with first-, second- and third-place votes and total points based on a 14-9-8-7-6-5-4-3-2-1 basis:

NAME, TEAM	1ST	2ND	3RD	POINTS
Barry Bonds, Giants	30	2	-	438
Sammy Sosa, Cubs	2	17	8	278
Luis Gonzalez, Diamondbacks	-	8	21	261
Albert Pujols, Cardinals	-	5	3	222
Lance Berkman, Astros	-	-	-	125

Pujols was also named the top National League rookie by *Baseball Weekly*, *The Sporting News*, and *Baseball Digest* and won the Players Choice Award as the top rookie in the league. His .610 slugging percentage earned him the NL Silver Slugger Award for the top slugging mark among third basemen.

Pujols was equally effective as a fielder and did whatever the team asked of him. He played four different positions—third base, left field, right field, and first base—and is believed to be the first major-leaguer to start thirty games at four different positions in a single season, though that statistic has never been verified.

"I'm not surprised I've had success because I worked hard for this," said Pujols. "God gave me the ability and talent to play this game. He gave me the ability and attitude to respect this game. It wouldn't be right for me to be lazy and take God's gifts for granted."[3]

The Cardinals' future never looked brighter.

CHAPTER SIX

Practice Makes Perfect

After winning many awards and cementing his place on the Cardinals' roster, Pujols could have relaxed a bit. He had made it. He had accomplished his childhood dreams. But being complacent is not a part of Pujols' nature. He wanted to become an even better baseball player.

"It's not what you did last year," he said. "It's what you're going to do this year. That's more important."[1]

Pujols set about to fine-tune his swing. He always has worked on his batting, but he was extra determined to have a strong year in his second season. Many reporters asked him if he could avoid the dreaded "sophomore jinx." Pujols dismissed those questions. The key to avoiding any kind of jinx would be to work ever harder.

HITTING AS AN ART AND A SCIENCE

For Pujols, perfecting his swing is a matter of repetition, patience, and confidence. But it is also a matter of learning. Listening and learning are big parts of what makes Pujols the great player he is.

"I'm a really smart player," Pujols explained. "If you tell me something, I get it quickly. If there is something wrong with my hitting, tell me what's

SEEING IS BELIEVING

What some players have said about Albert Pujols as a hitter:

"He caught my eye last season as a rookie when, against the Padres, he hit a home run on a three-ball, no-strike pitch—to the opposite field. Now that was something."

— Three-time NL batting champion Tony Gwynn

"I believe he's been reincarnated, that he played before, in the twenties and thirties, and he's back to prove something."

— Former teammate Mark McGwire, comparing Pujols to the legendary Babe Ruth

"I've never seen anything like it. He's so quick to the ball with his bat, he hits to all fields, he rarely goes out of the strike zone, and no situation seems to rattle him."

— Former Pirates manager Lloyd McClendon

"His approach is so mature at the plate. He doesn't get himself out."

— Cardinals teammate Scott Rolen

wrong and I'll pick it up right away. That's the best thing I have going for me, my ability to listen to a coach and fix what I'm doing wrong."[2]

Former Cardinals hitting coach Mitchell Page agrees with Pujols' assessment: "He has the best work habits I've ever seen out of a young kid. He takes nothing for granted."[3]

When Pujols enters the batter's box, the routine is always the same. He digs his right foot—the back foot for a right-handed batter like Pujols—into the ground to establish a good base. Then, he takes his bat and taps it on the back point of home plate. By doing so, he establishes his center of gravity and can be sure he has enough room to step into an outside pitch and get his bat on it.

Pujols does not think of these things when he prepares to bat. He just does them. Much like the skills it takes to ride a bike, these movements have become second nature to Pujols. "That's a habit I have," he says. "It doesn't make sense to explain it."[4]

With his placement in the batter's box established, Pujols then begins to assume his stance. He bends his knees and rocks back slightly so that more than half of his weight rests on his back foot. With the bat held upright, he begins his swinging motion. He shifts his weight forward, driving with his hips. Last is his actual bat swing. Perhaps nothing separates him from other hitters more than his incredible bat speed.

Jim Edmonds congratulates Albert Pujols on a home run against the Cincinnati Reds August 23, 2001.

When the whole rhythm and mechanics come together at the final moment of impact, the result is a sharply hit ball. To those who make a living coaching players how to properly hit a baseball, and especially to the fans, it is a thing of beauty.

"He's focused in everything he does, from hitting to running down the line," Cardinals Hall of Fame player and coach Red Schoendienst said. "He doesn't go through the motions."[5]

Pujols' swing may look so natural that the game appears easy to him. But the reality is he spends hours upon hours practicing his stance and his swing. It is hard work, but Pujols proves that hard work is rewarded.

"He has the ability to repeat his swing over and over and over, which leads to him being very consistent," said

RED KNOWS HITTING

Former St. Louis Cardinals player and coach Albert Fred "Red" Schoendienst knows a thing or two about hitting. Schoendienst played with the Cardinals, New York Giants, and Milwaukee Braves from 1945 to 1963 and was named an all-star in ten of his nineteen seasons. He hit .300 or better seven times and was known for his fine fielding as a second baseman.

Schoendienst managed the Cardinals from 1965 to 1976 as well as in 1980. He guided the team to the World Series twice, winning it in 1967. Incredibly, he served as a player, coach, or manager for forty-five straight years. Born in 1923 in Germantown, Illinois, Schoendienst was elected to the Hall of Fame in 1989 by the Veterans Committee.

Cardinals video coordinator Chad Blair, who has taped and charted all of Pujols' at-bats. "The adjustments he makes are tiny, minute. To have his swing that fine-tuned is amazing. That, coupled with a burning desire to be the baddest man on the planet swinging a bat for a living."[6]

When Pujols is at the top of his game, there is little doubt he is among the most feared hitters in baseball, perhaps the most feared. Aware of this, Pujols takes a confident but not cocky approach to the game.

"In my heart and mind, I know I can hit anybody," he said. "I'm always relaxed. It's hard to explain. It's like playing with my kids. It feels natural.

> **"The adjustments he makes are tiny, minute. To have his swing that fine-tuned is amazing. That, coupled with a burning desire to be the baddest man on the planet swinging a bat for a living."**
>
> **—Chad Blair**

Mark McGwire watches his record-setting home run in 1998.

"I don't know why people say I'm not supposed to be doing what I'm doing. I'm just trying to do my job. I'm blessed and I'm glad that I'm blessed."[7]

ADDED PRESSURE

As if he needed it, there was added pressure on Pujols entering his second season when Mark McGwire, one of the game's all-time best power hitters, decided to retire. McGwire began talking about retiring after the playoff loss to Arizona, but most people thought he would come back.

Though McGwire had to play through injuries in 2001 and batted only .187, he hit 29 home runs in 97 games. With 583 career home runs, he was only 17 away from joining Hank Aaron, Babe Ruth, and Willie Mays as the only players (at the time) to hit 600 career home runs or more. The

MARK MCGWIRE FILE
Full name: Mark David
    McGwire
Birthplace: Pomona, California
Height: 6'5"
Weight: 250 pounds
Date of birth: October 1, 1963
Bats: Right
Throws: Right
College: University of Southern
    California
Position: First baseman
MLB teams: Oakland Athletics
    (1986–1997), St. Louis
    Cardinals (1997–2001,
    retired)
MLB debut: August 22, 1986
Acquired: First round, tenth
    overall pick, 1984

> **"I believe I owe it to the Cardinals and the fans of St. Louis to step aside, so a talented free agent can be brought in as the final piece of what I expect can be a World Championship-caliber team."**
>
> **—Mark McGwire**

Cardinals gave every indication that they believed he would bounce back and were eager for him to continue his career. He was offered a $30 million extension to his contract prior to the 2001 season, and many news media outlets reported that the deal was done. However, there was a problem. McGwire never signed the contract.

"There's not a better sign of integrity in my opinion," said Cardinals manager Tony La Russa. "The man just walked away from $30 million. How many guys would do that?"[8]

In a prepared statement, McGwire said, "After considerable discussion with those closest to me, I have decided not to sign the extension, as I am unable to perform at a level equal to the salary the organization would be paying me. I believe I owe it to the Cardinals and the fans of St. Louis to step aside, so a talented free agent can be brought in as the final piece of what I expect can be a World Championship-caliber team."[9]

The news hit the Cardinals' players like a ton of bricks. The man who had been the heart and soul of the team since he arrived with the club in 1997 would actually be gone.

"It shocked me when I heard it last night," Pujols said at the time. "But it's something I'm sure the Cardinals will take care of. We've got a good general manager in Walt Jocketty and I'm sure he'll take care of it."[10]

In less than a year, Pujols went from a player fighting to earn a roster spot—one who a former coach said would have fun throwing the ball to McGwire at practice—to the man who would replace him. The time had come for Pujols to become the face of the Cardinals. And he was ready.

CHAPTER SEVEN

Overcoming Jinxes and Much More

With Mark McGwire officially retired, the Cardinals had the money to bring in some other players heading into 2002. They signed first baseman Tino Martinez and acquired closer Jason Isringhausen. They were also anxious to see how Woody Williams, acquired late in the 2001 season, could fit into the starting pitching rotation.

The new players lessened the loss of McGwire a little, but the Cardinals also needed Pujols to continue his great play from 2001. Pujols continued to be peppered with questions about a sophomore jinx.

A LEGENDARY VOICE

When Jack Buck died at age seventy-seven on June 18, 2002, Major League Baseball lost one of its most beloved broadcasters, one whose voice is entwined with some of the game's most memorable moments.

Cardinals fans fondly remember how he would end each St. Louis victory with his signature call: "That's a winner!" Among his many famous calls were Lou Brock's 3,000th hit and record-breaking 938th steal, Bob Gibson's no-hitter, and Mark McGwire's 61st home run on his way to the then-single-season record.

St. Louis fans still recite his call from Ozzie Smith's 1985 NLCS Game 5-winning home run: "Go crazy, folks! Go crazy!"

But of all his memorable calls, perhaps the most famous did not come during a Cardinals game. Buck called Game 1 of the 1988 World Series between the Los Angeles Dodgers and Oakland Athletics for CBS Radio. The Dodgers trailed 4–3 in the bottom of the ninth with two outs when manager Tommy Lasorda inserted an injured Kirk Gibson to pinch hit.

Facing future Hall of Fame closer Dennis Eckersley, Gibson battled back from an 0–2 count to a drama-filled full count. Then he smacked a golf-like swing into history.

"Unbelievable!" Buck shouted. "The Dodgers have won the game on a home run by Kirk Gibson. I don't believe what I just saw!"

The call, a radio call, is often mixed with the TV footage of a limping Gibson pumping his fist as he rounds second base in one of the most cherished moments in sports.

Buck's son, Joe, carries on the family tradition of broadcasting and is one of the top baseball and football announcers today.

Jack Buck interviews
Pujols April 25, 2001.

"Why do I get that question every day? I don't think there's pressure on me," he said. "I played every day last year. I just work hard every day and am happy to be in the lineup."[1]

Jinx or not, Pujols' season started slowly. He hit only 4 home runs in April. He hit 5 more home runs in May—not a bad start for most players but more was expected of Pujols. During the first part of the season, Pujols' batting average hovered around .280. Yet he was hitting the ball well with runners in scoring position and seemed ready to catch fire as he did as a rookie.

Meanwhile, the Cardinals were dealing with some off-field issues they never expected. On June 18, the team lost its beloved announcer, Jack Buck, to Parkinson's disease. The Hall of Famer had been in the hospital for more than two weeks, attempting to recover from surgeries for cancerous spots on his lung and kidney failure, both the effects of the disease. He was seventy-seven years old and had shared a special relationship with the Cardinals' players, fans, and baseball fans all over the world.

"The thing that amazes me about him—and all of us have our own styles—he understated things to the extent that they more than adequately conveyed what people saw and thought," said Marty Brennaman, Cincinnati Reds broadcaster and Hall of Famer. "When Kirk Gibson hit the home run off Dennis Eckersley to win the World Series game, he said seven words: 'I don't believe what I just saw!' And that conveyed everything that people in Dodger Stadium were thinking [and] people watching on TV or listening on the radio. He said it exactly the way it was. That's a talent that very few people like us in this business have. He was amazing. He never big-timed anybody. He never thought he was important. He was genuinely amazed at the following he has. He was special. He really was."[2]

"He was absolutely one of the greats in the business. I never saw a guy so wedded to the community as Jack in St. Louis."

—Gary Cohen

Mets broadcaster Gary Cohen agreed: "He was absolutely one of the greats in the business. I never saw a guy so wedded to the community as Jack in St. Louis. . . . He had a wonderful, self-deprecating personality and was just a fun guy to be around. He welcomed me and was always kind to me. He couldn't have been a better representative of the profession. He will be profoundly missed."[3]

Still reeling from the loss of Buck, the team was hit with more terrible news less than a week later. On June 22, Cards pitcher Darryl Kile was found dead in the team hotel on a road trip to Chicago. The thirty-three-year-old Kile died of a heart condition in his sleep. The organization was deeply grieving.

"Our club is just totally staggered, I mean, devastated," Cardinals manager Tony La Russa said, wiping away tears, when he learned of the news.[4]

Kile left behind his wife, Flynn, and five-year-old twins.

"This has been a very difficult week with the loss of Jack Buck and now the loss of Darryl Kile," Cardinals general manager Walt Jocketty said. "It is going to be a real tough period for the Cardinals organization and the citizens of St. Louis."[5]

A SAD DAY

Deaths of active baseball players have been rare through the years. The deaths of Thurman Munson and Roberto Clemente are perhaps the most remembered.

Munson was the team captain for the New York Yankees when he died in a plane crash on August 2, 1979. Clemente also died in a plane crash. The Pittsburgh Pirates Hall of Famer was delivering relief supplies to Nicaragua on December 31, 1972, when his plane crashed. On October 11, 2006, Yankees pitcher Cory Lidle died when his small plane crashed into a building in New York City.

MOVING ON

The Cardinals had no choice but to continue playing baseball. With heavy hearts, they took the field and played. And they played well.

Pujols found his rhythm and began hitting like the player who took the baseball world by storm in 2001. The pitching staff came together and the team regrouped to win the National League Central with a 97–65 record. Outfielder Jim Edmonds developed into a leader, and a trade with the Philadelphia Phillies brought third baseman Scott Rolen as the missing piece.

The real key, however, was Pujols. After the All-Star break, he hit .335 for the remainder of the season with a league-leading 61 RBIs.

When the playoffs arrived, the Cardinals found themselves facing a familiar

THIS TIME IT COUNTS

The 2003 All-Star Game made history as the first of its kind with real meaning. After the 2002 game ended in a tie due to both teams running out of pitchers, Major League Baseball decided to put something on the line for the Midsummer Classic.

Starting with the 2003 game, the winning league would earn home-field advantage for its World Series representative. The slogan for 2003 read, "This Time It Counts."

The American League won the game 7–6, which earned home field for the eventual AL champion New York Yankees. The National League's Florida Marlins, however, defeated the Yankees for the World Series title in Game 6 at Yankee Stadium.

foe—the Arizona Diamondbacks, the team that eliminated St. Louis the year before. But this time, the series belonged to St. Louis.

Pujols played an important part in the series, a three-game NLDS sweep. He went 2-for-4 in the first game with 2 RBIs and 2 runs scored. He finished the series with a .300 batting average.

Next up was the NLCS and a date with Barry Bonds' San Francisco Giants. A berth in the World Series was on the line. Pujols hit a home run in the first game, but San Francisco won 9–6. Giants shortstop Rich Aurilia hit 2 home runs in the second game, a 4–1 San Francisco win that pushed the Giants' lead to 2–0 in the best-of-seven series.

The Cardinals pulled out a 5–4 win in Game 3 thanks to solo home runs by Eli Marrero, Mike Matheny, and Edmonds. St. Louis continued to fight hard in the series, but the timely hits belonged to San Francisco.

In Game 4, San Francisco's Benito Santiago hit a 2-run homer in the bottom of the eighth inning in a 4–3 Giants victory. It was a game the Cardinals sorely needed. Only three teams had been able to rebound from a 3–1 playoff deficit since the best-of-seven format was introduced in 1985. The Cardinals' World Series dreams were fading. "We went out ready to play," said Pujols. "We actually got a lot of hits but we didn't get the big hit."[6]

Pujols tosses his bat as he watches his home run.

St. Louis was determined not to give up, however. Matt Morris pitched brilliantly in Game 5. He went eight and two-thirds innings but took the loss when Kenny Loften singled in David Bell off Steve Kline in the bottom of the ninth inning for a 2–1 victory.

The Giants were going to the World Series, and the roller-coaster season for the Cardinals had ended. St. Louis had been through many ups and downs in 2002, from the deaths of Buck and Kile to the brink of the World Series. The emotions came out in the locker room after the loss.

> **"What we had to go through this year, you can't help but be proud of the guys and the way we battled and showed our character."**
>
> **—Dave Veres**

"There's no doubt it's a special team," said reliever Dave Veres, who was Kile's best friend on the team. "But we still wanted to go a little bit further. What we overcame was amazing. What we had to go through this year, you can't help but be proud of the guys and the way we battled and showed our character."[7]

The city of St. Louis had suffered a lot in 2002, but the Cardinals gave their fans reason to smile. That was not lost on team chairman Frederick O. Hanser.

"Sometimes when you go down to a bitter defeat like this, what you have is how proud you are of the team and how well they did," he said. "If you go on to win the World Series, of course you're proud of them. But somehow the bitterness of this defeat brings out the incredible character of these guys and how well they've performed all year long under adversity, bouncing back. It's just a tremendous achievement."[8]

Pujols had a hit in every NLCS game but did not drive in any runs after Game 1. He finished the series with a .263 average. The series did not turn out as he would have liked, but 2002 was another huge success for the young superstar.

Not only did Pujols avoid the "sophomore slump," he again led the team in nearly every offensive category. He batted .314 with 34 home runs, 127 RBIs, and 118 runs scored, leading the club in all four categories for a second straight season. He became the first player in MLB history to hit at least .300 with 30 home runs, 100 RBIs, and 100 runs scored in his first two seasons and finished second to Barry Bonds for the National League MVP award.

A BATTING TITLE TO CALL HIS OWN

The Cardinals had plenty of hitting power entering 2003. The real question was whether their pitching could hold up. It did not. When Morris missed a

Pujols touches second base as Jeff Kent reaches for the late throw. Second-base umpire Dan Iassogna watches the play.

large part of the season with an elbow injury, the pitching staff collapsed, and St. Louis fell out of playoff contention.

Pujols, however, had a brilliant season despite playing with an elbow injury. His throwing was limited, but he hit the ball extremely well. For a while, it appeared he might even flirt with a .400 batting average for the season.

CHASING "TEDDY BALLGAME"

Boston Red Sox legend Ted Williams is the last player to hit .400 for a season. He did it in 1941 and did it in style. Entering the last day of the season with an average of .3996, the team offered to let him sit out the game and secure the milestone because his average would round up to .400. But Williams, also known as the "Splendid Splinter," decided to play. He played in the doubleheader, getting 6 hits in 8 at-bats to raise his season batting average to .406.

Williams was elected to the Hall of Fame in 1966 with a career batting average of .344 and 521 home runs. He died in 2002. No player since Williams has hit .400 in a season. A few have flirted with the magical number, most notably the Kansas City Royals' George Brett, who hit .390 in 1980.

He eventually cooled down but not much. When the season was over, Pujols' numbers were eye-popping: a .359 average with 43 home runs, 124 RBIs, and 137 runs scored. He also collected 212 hits with 51 doubles. Along the way, he hit safely in thirty consecutive games, the most by a Cardinal since Stan Musial hit safely in thirty straight games in 1950.

Pujols and Musial share second place for the club record behind Rogers Hornsby, who hit safely in thirty-three straight games in 1922.

"Any time you're [mentioned] with those guys, you're talking about Hall of Famers," Pujols said. "When you get your name out there with Stan Musial, you're talking about the best hitter who ever played for the Cardinals organization."[9]

Pujols' .359 average was tops in the league, earning him the NL batting crown. At twenty-three, he became the youngest NL batting champion since

HOME RUN DERBY THRILLS

During the 2003 All-Star festivities, Albert Pujols wowed the crowd at Chicago's U.S. Cellular Field with an awesome performance during the Home Run Derby. Pujols eliminated defending champion Jason Giambi in the semifinals by tying the then-record 14 home runs in a round.

In the finals, Pujols faced Garret Anderson of the Anaheim Angels. Anderson won the derby by narrowly bettering Pujols 9–8. On the day, Pujols actually hit more home runs than Anderson, 26–22.

"I couldn't be more happy," Pujols said graciously. "It would be nice if I had won it, but I'm happy for Anderson. He hit one more home run than me. That's what it's all about."

Los Angeles' Tommy Davis in 1962. He also improved his string of hitting at least .300 with 30 home runs, 100 RBIs, and 100 runs scored to three straight seasons.

By now Pujols' name was showing up all over the record book. With 114 home runs through his first three seasons, he tied Ralph Kiner's major-league record for most home runs through any player's first three years. He also became just the third player, along with Jose Canseco and McGwire, to hit thirty or more home runs in each of his first three seasons.

Individually, Pujols was at the top of his game. But statistics never meant much to Pujols. He wanted more. He wanted to play in the World Series.

Pujols celebrates after crossing home plate.

8

Pujols' Dream: The World Series

The St. Louis Cardinals had a terrific season in 2004. They breezed through the regular season with a 105–57 record, tops in baseball. They had no problem securing the NL Central title, winning the race by thirteen games. Things had been so easy that the team rested many of its players during the final month. The big division lead was a blessing since the rest allowed many of the Cardinals' injured players to heal in time for the postseason.

Pujols points to the dugout after hitting a home run.

When the playoffs finally arrived, all eight of the Cardinals' position players were healthy, and the NLDS matchup with the Los Angeles Dodgers was no contest. St. Louis only lost one game in the series, winning the best-of-five race in four games. In the first game, the Cards' power was on display as the offense tied the NLDS record with 5 home runs.

A BIG PAY DAY

In February 2004, the St. Louis Cardinals decided they had seen enough of Albert Pujols to know they wanted him to remain on their team for a very long time. The club gave Pujols a seven-year, $100 million contract, making him the ninth MLB player to receive a $100 million contract. The deal was the largest the Cardinals had ever offered a player.

"This deal not only recognizes Albert for his accomplishments over the past three seasons but, all along, we felt that it was important to retain a player such as Albert who came up through our farm system, and see to it that he remained a part of the club's nucleus well into the future," said Cardinals general manager Walt Jocketty.

St. Louis surged out to a 2–0 lead in the NLCS against the Houston Astros. Albert Pujols reached base four times in Game 1 and came up huge in Game 2 with a home run in the eighth inning to break a 4–4 tie. The Cardinals' World Series dreams began to fade,

Pujols hits a home run against the Astros.

however, as the Astros responded with three straight wins at Minute Maid Park in Houston. The Cards were heading home to Busch Stadium. Though Houston had stolen the momentum in the series, St. Louis was confident it could get the job done.

"It's going to be good," Cardinals relief pitcher Kiko Calero said. "We need two wins to go to the World Series, and we can do it. We won the first two games there, and there's no reason we can't do it now. We have good hitters, and [pitcher Matt] Morris will be ready."[1]

TWO GAMES, TWO MAGICAL NIGHTS

Morris did not have his best stuff in Game 6 but was able to give the Cards 5 innings, allowing 3 runs on 5 hits. He gave up a run in the first inning, but the team quickly got it back when Pujols hit a 2-run homer in the bottom of the inning.

Pujols added a double in the third inning and scored. St. Louis held a 4–3 lead after four innings, and the lead looked like it

IT IS GONE—AGAIN AND AGAIN

On July 20 in Chicago, Albert Pujols had the best day of his career. He sparked the Cardinals' rally from a 7–1 deficit to an eventual 11–8 victory by hitting 3 home runs. It was the first time in his career he hit 3 homers in a game. He finished the game with 5 hits, 5 RBIs, 15 total bases, and 5 runs scored.

"It was the first time I've hit three home runs and it came at the right time," Pujols said. "It's one of those days you never forget."

would hold up. But the Astros scored the tying run in the ninth inning, sending the do-or-die game for the Cardinals into extra innings.

The Astros' Craig Biggio dives toward first base past the attempted tag by Pujols May 29, 2004, in Houston. Biggio was called safe on the play.

Neither team scored in the 10th and 11th innings. In the bottom of the 12th, Pujols led off. Astros reliever Dan Miceli was careful not to give Pujols too good of a pitch, one that Pujols could drive out of the park to end the game. Pujols remained patient and wound up on first base with a walk. Scott Rolen then popped up, setting the scene for Jim Edmonds.

Miceli delivered the pitch. Whack! The crowd roared as the ball shot off Edmonds' bat. Four hundred and five feet later, the ball landed in the St. Louis bullpen behind right field. The fans at Busch Stadium went into hysterics as Pujols and Edmonds rounded the bases. The 6–4 victory meant the Cardinals survived elimination and would play another game.

WALKING OFF INTO HISTORY

Jim Edmonds' 12th-inning walk-off home run in Game 6 of the NLCS marked the sixth time in history that a walk-off homer was hit in NLCS play. Houston's Jeff Kent became the fifth slugger to do it in Game 5 of the same series.

PLAYER	TEAM	OPPONENT	YEAR	GAME
Johnny Bench	Cincinnati Reds	New York Mets	1973	Game 1
Steve Garvey	San Diego Padres	Chicago Cubs	1984	Game 4
Ozzie Smith	St. Louis Cardinals	Los Angeles Dodgers	1985	Game 5
Lenny Dkystra	New York Mets	Houston Astros	1986	Game 3
Jeff Kent	Houston Astros	St. Louis Cardinals	2004	Game 5
Jim Edmonds	St. Louis Cardinals	Houston Astros	2004	Game 6

"I was just trying to get a hit, actually," said Edmonds. "Obviously, [Pujols] deserves all the respect in the world. [Miceli] kind of wasn't trying to give him anything to hit. I figured if I could hit something hard in the gap or get another base hit, he would run hard to get to third and we would get a chance to score somehow.

"So that's it. I was just looking for a ball to get a good swing at. I wasn't trying to go deep. I was trying to hit the ball hard. Thank God for that. We get to play tomorrow."[2]

There are few things more exciting in sports than a decisive Game 7. When a league championship series pushes to a Game 7, the drama is thick as fog. One team's dreams come to an end, while another team celebrates.

In Game 7, St. Louis found itself trailing 2–1 heading into the bottom of the sixth. It could have been a bigger hole had Edmonds not made a spectacular, diving catch in the outfield to prevent more Houston runs. The Cards needed a big hit, and Pujols was up to the task.

Facing a 1–2 count, Pujols smashed a double down the left-field line to drive home the tying run. On the very next pitch, Scott Rolen launched a home run to give St. Louis a 4–2 lead. The team tacked on another run in the eighth but did not need it. The lead was large enough for a 5–2 victory.

IT'S IN THE GAME

Albert Pujols appeared on the cover of EA Sports' popular *MVP Baseball 2004* video game.

"It's a thrill for me to be a part of a game that offers fans the authentic look and feel of stepping up to the plate and standing in the batter's box," said Pujols. "There is science to hitting that is hard to recreate, but that's exactly what EA Sports has done in *MVP Baseball* 2004."

While filming a commercial for the game with Pujols, Cardinals manager Tony La Russa revealed that his players play video games regularly, and the EA Sports *MVP Baseball* series is one of their favorites.

"It's the one guys enjoy the most," said La Russa. "There's a time to work and a time to relax, and when it's time to relax, a lot of guys do it [play *MVP Baseball*]. They'll have competitions—they have a lot of fun with it, and it's kind of fun to watch them having fun."

Needing two wins in a row, the Cardinals had done it. Pujols and his team were headed to the World Series. It marked the first time St. Louis had made a World Series appearance since 1987, and it hoped to capture its first championship since 1982.

"It's amazing," said Pujols. This is what you dream about, you know . . . going to the World Series."[3]

Pujols was named the NLCS MVP. During the series, he batted. 500 (14-for-28) with 4 home runs,

9 RBIs, and 10 runs scored. He set NLCS records for total hits and total bases with 28.

Meanwhile, some magic was happening in the other championship series. The Boston Red Sox had accomplished the unthinkable by overcoming a 3–0 New York Yankees series lead to win the ALCS 4–3. The Red Sox had not won the World Series since 1918, but the 2004 Red Sox were a team that believed in itself as much as the Cardinals believed in themselves. This World Series had the makings to be one for the ages.

"[The Red Sox] showed what they can do, coming back from 3–0," said Pujols. "They never give up, they knew it wasn't over until they lose that fourth game."[4]

A BITTER END

Somehow, the magic of the Cardinals' 2004 season evaporated in the World Series. Many felt this Series would be one of the greatest ever, but the only greatness came from the Red Sox. St. Louis never led in any game as Boston rolled to four straight victories to claim the championship.

OLD FRIENDS MEET AGAIN
The 2004 World Series between the St. Louis Cardinals and Boston Red Sox marked the third time the two clubs met for baseball's championship. The two teams also met in 1946 and 1967 with the Cardinals winning both series 4–3.

The usually potent Cardinals' bats were mostly silent, and the team even made some uncharacteristic base-running mistakes. They needed to play their best to defeat the Red Sox, but they did not play anything near their best.

"I'm disappointed that we didn't play well in the World Series just for the sake of the people, and to hear that crowd go crazy again," said Edmonds, who managed only one hit during the Series. "That's tough. We didn't even give them a chance to cheer."[5]

Pujols batted .333 (5-for-15) in the four games. But the timely hits that helped St. Louis to baseball's best record were lacking in the World Series. During the final three games of the Series, the Cardinals went only 1-for-18 with runners in scoring position.

"If you've been following our team all year long, five or six or seven runs is not enough," Pujols said. "You have to make 27 outs. We can put runs up in a

A CURE FOR THE CURSE

When the Boston Red Sox defeated the St. Louis Cardinals in the 2004 World Series, the team put to rest the "Curse of the Bambino." The supposed curse hung over the Red Sox since the team traded Babe Ruth, also known as the Bambino, to the New York Yankees.

The Red Sox had won five of the first fifteen World Series, including the 1918 championship with Ruth as a pitcher, but they did not win another one after the trade for eighty-six years. Meanwhile, the Yankees became one of the best franchises in all of sports.

Albert Pujols sits in the dugout during Game 4 of the 2004 World Series against the Boston Red Sox.

hurry. It didn't happen in this series, but we need to get over it."[6]

Though disappointed they did not win the World Series, there was much for the Cardinals to be proud of in 2004. Pujols, as usual, did his part. He batted

.331 with 46 home runs, 123 RBIs, and 51 doubles. He also lead the league with 133 runs scored. Rolen and Edmonds also were outstanding. The trio combined for 122 home runs and 358 RBIs. The three power hitters were dubbed "MV3" because they all had put up MVP-caliber numbers.

The actual MVP went to San Francisco's Barry Bonds. Pujols, Rolen, and Edmonds finished third, fourth, and fifth in the voting. Pujols would have enjoyed winning the MVP award. However, with the World Series loss still stinging, he was more interested in the future.

> **"I choose to look forward to my dreams instead of any successes I might have had in the past."**
>
> **—Albert Pujols**

"Your mind can get distracted by things that happened in the past that you can't make better anyway, right?" he said. "If you are driven to be the best you can be, whatever happened in the past is over—and there's nothing you can do [about it]. I guess you can say that I choose to look forward to my dreams instead of any successes I might have had in the past."[7]

Another chance at a world championship was in Pujols' and the Cardinals' future.

CHAPTER NINE

Building a Foundation

Of all of Albert Pujols' awe-inspiring hits, perhaps the one that will make the biggest impact was one he launched on May 5, 2005. On that day, Pujols and his wife, Deidre, formally introduced the Pujols Family Foundation, a charitable organization designed to help people afflicted with Down syndrome and their families.

"I want to hit a grand slam off the field," Pujols said at a press conference at the Cardinals Club inside Busch Stadium. "It wasn't something we started on our own. It was something that God showed us. The foundation is dedicated to sharing our commitment to faith, family and others."[1]

DEIDRE PH

Pujols and Deidre announce the Pujols Family Foundation.

Pujols and Deidre knew firsthand the effects of Down syndrome because their daughter Isabella has the disease. They knew the difficulties the disease creates and what stresses it can put on a family. And they had always believed in charitable causes. It was only a matter of time before their beliefs, desires, and ambitions to help others combined into a powerful force. Meeting Todd Perry pulled it all together.

Perry had dreams of starting a foundation. Believing the Pujols family would be the perfect partner, he gave Deidre, also known as Dee Dee, a thirty-minute presentation. Deidre silently and intently listened.

"Then she looked up and said, 'This is what I've been praying for,'" said Perry, the executive director of the foundation. "I got chills. Dee Dee knew she wanted to help others, but she didn't know how. I knew how. I just married our two ideas."[2]

BREAKFAST OF CHAMPIONS

Some of the most famous athletes in sports history have been selected by Wheaties to be on the front of its cereal boxes. Through the years, many baseball greats such as Babe Ruth, Joe DiMaggio, Ted Williams, Stan Musial, and Mickey Mantle have received the honor. In 2005, Albert Pujols was added to the impressive list.

"It's a great honor for me to be on the cover of the Wheaties box," Pujols said. "I'm very excited about sharing the Wheaties box with my family."

The first athlete to appear on a Wheaties box was New York Yankees first baseman Lou Gehrig in 1934.

The foundation began to pick up steam quickly. With Pujols' popularity and Deidre's passion to drive the foundation to new heights, lives were being affected for the good.

The Down Syndrome Association of Greater St. Louis felt the effects immediately. Deidre and Pujols had already lent their time and energy and had made some donations to the association before the launch of their own foundation. But the foundation was able to bring the association to a higher level.

Formerly run by volunteers, the Down Syndrome Association now has the means to help many families it could not assist before. It even has a salaried executive director. One of the association's main fund-raisers, the Buddy Walk, has been moved to Busch Stadium due to its growth. The event, which drew sixty walkers in its first year in 1996, now boasts more than 3,500.

"Dee Dee's giving is endless," said Beth Schroeder, former president of the Down Syndrome Association of Greater St. Louis. "Whether she gets in front of a TV camera, clarifies misconceptions about Down syndrome or plans the menu for a fund-raiser, her support is unbelievable."[3]

Deidre, who serves as the president of the foundation, gives countless interviews and guest-speaker appearances promoting the causes of the foundation as well as faith in God. It creates a hectic schedule for a mother of three, but it is a labor of love.

"We can retire, and we can rest when we get to heaven," said Deidre. "I mean now is the time God has put us in a position of power. I mean of great power. I believe in speaking out on his behalf and really speaking out on what is right."[4]

SWINGING FOR CHARITY

One of the foundation's most popular events is the annual Pujols Family Foundation Golf Classic. The event raises awareness about Down syndrome and raises a considerable amount of money for charity, as

GOING ONCE, GOING TWICE . . . SOLD

In addition to holding auctions at his annual charity golf event, Albert Pujols likes to attend other auctions, too. But unlike those who seek to fill their showcases with unique items, Pujols simply likes to spend his money on worthwhile causes.

He once bid $2,500 for the glove that pitcher Roger Clemens wore when he pitched his 300th victory. After his bid won the glove, he gave it—along with a hug—to a teenager with Down syndrome. Another time, at an auction to benefit children with Down syndrome, Pujols won two Florida vacation packages, priced at $3,000 each, and promptly gave them to children right there at the auction.

Sometimes, there might not be an obvious choice for who should receive the items on which he bids. So, Pujols does the next best thing. His $5,000 bid for an autographed Chris Carpenter jersey was the highest at the St. Louis chapter of the Baseball Writers' Association of America auction. When his bid was declared the winner, he handed the jersey to the person with the next highest bid.

well. The third annual event, held in 2005, raised more than $200,000. The fourth event, held in 2006, was believed to have generated even more than that.

"This is what it's all about," Pujols said. "God gave me an opportunity, and I feel blessed to take advantage of every opportunity I have."[5]

Many of Pujols' Cardinals teammates participate. St. Louis manager Tony La Russa also participates, as do several former Cardinals players and staff. La Russa said, "That's a good organization. They had some great volunteers, just the nicest people. And the kids . . . it makes you glad you did it when you meet all those kids afterwards."[6]

An auction is also part of the event. Some of the memorabilia at the 2006 event included signed items from LaDainian Tomlinson, Torry Holt, Marshall Faulk, Wayne Gretzky, David Wright, and musician Chuck Berry as well as several items from Pujols.

HAIL! HAIL! ROCK 'N' ROLL
Chuck Berry, one of the most instrumental forces behind the birth of rock and roll music, was born in St. Louis on October 18, 1926. Born Charles Edward Anderson Berry, he produced chart-topping hits such as "Maybellene," "Roll Over Beethoven," "Rock and Roll Music," and "Sweet Little Sixteen." He was among the first musicians inducted into the Rock and Roll Hall of Fame in 1986.

INTERNATIONAL DREAMS

The second part of the Pujols Family Foundation's goal is to help poor children and families in Pujols' native land of the Dominican Republic.

"The reason we want to help outside of the United States is because obviously Albert is from the Dominican Republic," said Deidre. "These are his people and he cares about them as much as anybody here locally in St. Louis. It's important we share his heart and our family's heart with the Dominican people."[7]

The Pujols family took a trip to the Dominican Republic to scout out where they could help most. In 2005, the foundation chose to support the Orfanato Niños de Christo orphanage in Santo Domingo.

Through the foundation, the orphanage has received more than five hundred pounds (two hundred twenty-seven kilograms) of school supplies, more than 1,000 pairs of shoes, and many other necessities. During a 2005 Christmas event—one that raised more than $120,000 for the foundation—the

AN APPLE A DAY . . .

Apple Vacations, a travel company, showed it believed in the mission of the Pujols Family Foundation by partnering with the organization in a unique way. Apple Vacations announced it would provide free round-trip air transportation for medical professionals and foundation staff members from St. Louis to Punta Cana International airport in the Dominican Republic.

Pujols enjoys himself while warming up for a 2005 game.

orphanage received a special surprise when Ford Motor Company donated an eighteen-seat van. The moment was so emotional that a representative from the orphanage was moved to tears.

"When you see Albert around these kids, it is hard to believe he is the same person who everyone talks about being so serious at the park," said Perry. "He always has a big smile. He will get down and roll around on the ground with them. There are always high-fives and hugs for everyone. He is a big kid again."[8]

"When you see Albert around these kids, it is hard to believe he is the same person who everyone talks about being so serious at the park."

—Todd Perry

Pujols' desire to hit a grand slam off the field has certainly cleared the fence. And there is no telling how many lives will be affected in the future.

"The beauty of this thing is that we're going to share our faith," said Pujols. "That's our main goal. That we can get to those people and not just write a check for whatever they need, but at the same time share with them what the Lord has done in our lives."[9]

10
An MVP Season

Entering the 2005 season, Albert Pujols had accomplished almost everything he could in professional baseball. He had become one of the game's top players and had played in a World Series. He had hauled in almost every award available—except an MVP award, that is.

The St. Louis Cardinals needed to shake off their sluggish performance in the 2004 World Series, a four-game sweep at the hands of the Boston Red Sox. With Pujols to lead the way, that proved to be no problem.

Despite battling a foot injury throughout the season, Pujols was once again amazing at the plate. He finished in the top five in the National League in all three Triple Crown categories. He ranked second in batting average at .330, third in home runs with 41, and tied for second in RBIs with 117. He was also second in the league with 360 total bases and fourth in hits with 195. Pujols made his fourth All-Star Game appearance in five years.

In the National League Divisional Series, St. Louis faced the San Diego Padres. The series was no contest, however. The Cardinals won three straight in relatively easy fashion. Pujols went 5-for-9 with 2 RBIs in the series, collecting a hit, a walk, and scoring a run in each game. But the real hero was Reggie Sanders, who set a National League Divisional Series record with 10 RBIs, including a grand slam in Game 1.

A HITTER WITH A HEART

During a 2005 game at Busch Stadium, Albert Pujols hit a hard foul ball into the stands. The ball hit a two-year-old child named Bryson King in the forehead. The child screamed in pain and was rushed to a hospital where it was learned he suffered a mild skull fracture.

Before the child was released from the hospital, a special visitor showed up to make sure he was all right. It was Pujols. And he came with a variety of gifts for the young boy. Pujols brought Bryson an autographed wooden baseball bat, an autographed Cardinals hat, an autographed baseball card, two autographed baseballs, and other memorabilia. Pujols also posed for a photograph and offered the boy's parents tickets to any game they would like to come see.

"I'm just here to pay the family some respect," Pujols said. "I'm glad he's doing better. He's a nice little kid."

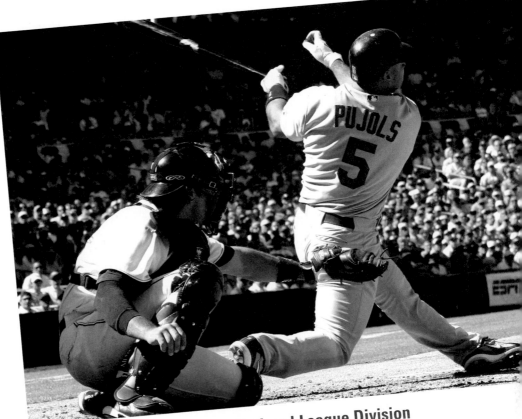

Pujols hits a home run in the National League Division Series game October 3, 2006, in San Diego.

"He really lit it up for us," Cardinals manager Tony La Russa said of Sanders. "He was the guy that provided the margin where it wasn't quite as scary. I think Reggie, you know, he fits in. One of the things we believe about our club is that we have a bunch of guys that are prime-timers. They're not afraid to take big at-bats. He's one of them."[1]

The sweep meant another National League Championship Series for St. Louis, marking the team's third appearance in the series in Pujols' five years with the club. The Cardinals' opposition was the Houston Astros, a team they knew very well.

ALMOST, BUT NOT QUITE

The Cardinals knew the National League Championship Series matchup with the Astros was going to be a tough task, and they struck first. Sanders hit a 2-run homer in the first inning of Game 1 as the Cards scored a 5–3 victory.

Houston responded, however, with three straight wins, finding just enough to win very tight games. The Astros won Game 2, 4–1, before sending the series to Houston. There, the Astros managed to win a pair of one-run games and claim a 3–1 lead in the series.

ALL IN THE FAMILY

Hoping the ability to hit a baseball a long way runs in the Pujols family genes, the St. Louis Cardinals used a sixth-round pick in the 2005 First-Year Player Draft to select Wilfrido Pujols, Albert's first cousin. Like Albert, Wilfrido attended Fort Osage High School in the Kansas City area.

St. Louis was in desperate need of a spark and found itself facing elimination in the ninth inning of Game 5. The Cardinals trailed 4–2 and were down to their last out. Their hopes rested with Pujols, who stepped to the plate with David Ecsktein and Jim Edmonds on base. Pujols was 0-for-4 during the game and had already left four runners on base. He had hoped for one more chance, and he got it.

Houston pitcher Brad Lidge threw a hanging slider, and Pujols swung. Crack! The Houston fans at Minute Maid Park fell silent as the ball leaped from Pujols' bat. It kept rising and did not touch down until it had traveled 412 feet and over the train tracks in left field.

"I didn't know if I should let go of the bat or take it with me," said Pujols. "I was shocked. I put my best swing of the night, and I didn't know what to do as I was running the bases."[2]

The 3-run blast was Pujols' 10th postseason home run in his career and gave St. Louis a 5–4 lead. When the Astros failed to score in the bottom of the inning, the dream of returning to the World Series was still alive for the Cardinals.

"It was awesome," outfielder Larry Walker said of Pujols' dramatic homer. "We all jumped up. There was more noise in our dugout than in the whole stadium at that moment. It was fun to be out there and be part of it."[3]

St. Louis' dream came crashing down in Game 6, however, as Houston notched a 5–1 win to take the series 4–2. The game marked the end of an era in St. Louis as it was the final one in beloved Busch

Stadium. The team began play in a new stadium, also called Busch Stadium, in 2006. It was built right next door to the old Busch Stadium.

Not long after the final out was registered, St. Louis fans began to chant "Let's Go Cardinals" as a tribute to the team and as a farewell to the stadium they called home for forty years. In that time, six World Series and eight National League Championship Series had been played there.

When asked what he would miss most about the old Busch Stadium, Pujols said, "Everything man. The fans, the players, the home runs I hit here, all the moments we had here the last two weeks of the season with every Hall of Famer coming through and the future Hall of Famers."[4]

THE MOMENT FINALLY ARRIVES

With the season done and the Chicago White Sox winners against the Houston Astros in the World

WORTH THE WAIT

In 2005, the Chicago White Sox joined the 2004 Boston Red Sox as teams that ended very long droughts between World Series championships. The Red Sox had gone eighty-six years between titles. When the White Sox defeated the Houston Astros in the 2005 World Series, it marked their first championship in eighty-eight years. Both teams won their long-awaited championships in World Series sweeps.

FIRSTS IN THE NEW BUSCH STADIUM

Groundbreaking:	January 17, 2004
Inaugural game:	April 10, 2006
Opponent:	Milwaukee Brewers
Ceremonial first pitches:	Chris Carpenter and Albert Pujols to Bob Gibson and Willie McGee
First pitch:	3:14 p.m., Mark Mulder to Brady Clark
First Cardinals hit:	David Eckstein, second inning, April 10, 2006
First Cardinals home run:	Albert Pujols, third inning, April 10, 2006

Series, there was only one matter left to close the 2005 campaign: the naming of the MVP. On November 15, 2005, the votes were counted, and the announcement was made.

Albert Pujols was the National League MVP.

Pujols received eighteen of the thirty-two first-place votes, bettering runner-up Andruw Jones of the Atlanta Braves by twenty-seven points.

"This is a great moment," Pujols said. "Fans and my family and friends were waiting. I'm still going to hear a lot of phone calls from friends. I still need to call some friends down in the Dominican who are just as proud as the city of St. Louis. There are some people in the Dominican that are pretty excited that I received this award."[5]

THE DREAM COMES TRUE

By the end of April 2006, the Cardinals boasted a stunning record in their beautiful new home, the brand new Busch Stadium. Their 17–8 record marked the best season start in the history of the team. By May 12, the Cardinals owned the top spot in the NL Central.

The rest of the season would prove to be a struggle. Injuries plagued the team's stars, including Pujols. A muscle strain in June put Pujols on the disabled list for the first time in his career. Yet the team soldiered on. The Cardinals suffered through three losing streaks of seven or more games, but a big division lead early in the season helped them. Though the Cardinals went 66–70 after May 12, they never gave up their spot atop the NL Central. Pujols did his part, hitting .331 with career highs in RBIs (137) and home runs (49).

ST. LOUIS CARDINALS' MOST VALUABLE PLAYER WINNERS

1925 - Rogers Hornsby

1926 - Bob O'Farrell

1928 - Jim Bottomley

1931 - Frankie Frisch

1934 - Dizzy Dean

1937 - Joe Medwick

1942 - Mort Cooper

1943 - Stan Musial

1944 - Marty Marion

1946 - Stan Musial

1948 - Stan Musial

1964 - Ken Boyer

1967 - Orlando Cepeda

1968 - Bob Gibson

1971 - Joe Torre

1979 - Keith Hernandez

1985 - Willie McGee

2005 - Albert Pujols

Albert Pujols hits a double in the fourth inning against the Detroit Tigers during Game 3 of the 2006 World Series.

In the NLDS, St. Louis beat the San Diego Padres for the second straight year. After defeating San Diego three games to one, the Cardinals advanced to the NLCS where they faced the New York Mets. The best-of-seven series went right to the wire. With the teams knotted at three games each, they met for the deciding game in New York. With the teams tied 1–1 going into the ninth, the Cardinals' Yadier Molina slammed a 2-run homer at the top of the inning.

The Mets were not ready to concede defeat, however. In the bottom of the inning, trailing 3–1, the Mets loaded the bases. With two outs, Mets' slugger Carlos Beltran came to the plate. Pitcher Adam Wainwright remained cool. He struck out Beltran to end the game and send the Cardinals to the World Series against the Detroit Tigers.

With his son A.J. on his shoulders, Pujols holds on to the World Series trophy with Walt Jocketty (center) and Tony La Russa.

While the Cardinals may have struggled at the end of the regular season, they were red hot in the postseason. The World Series was no exception. They made quick work of the Tigers. The Cardinals lost just one game, claiming the title of world champions after Game 5 at home in St. Louis. Along with his teammates, Pujols had reached the top of the baseball world in front of the hometown fans.

"Now I can say I have a World Series ring in my trophy case," Pujols said. "And that's what you play for. It doesn't matter how much money you make or what kind of numbers you put up in the big leagues. If you walk out of this game and you don't have a ring, you haven't accomplished everything."[6]

But Pujols would accomplish even more. On November 3, he was awarded his first Gold Glove. Pujols had long been recognized for his strengths as a hitter. Now he was honored for his fielding, too.

Yet the biggest award was still to come. On November 8, Pujols received the Marvin Miller Man of the Year Award from the MLB Players Association. The award is given to the MLB player whose performance on the field and contributions to the community inspire others to higher levels of achievement. Pujols was honored for being a hero off the field as well as on it.

CAREER STATISTICS

Albert Pujols' career batting statistics

YEAR	TEAM	G	AB	R	H	2B
2001	St. Louis	161	590	112	194	47
2002	St. Louis	157	590	118	185	40
2003	St. Louis	157	591	137	212	51
2004	St. Louis	154	592	133	196	51
2005	St. Louis	161	591	129	195	38
2006	St. Louis	143	535	119	177	33
2007	St. Louis	158	565	99	185	38
Total		1,091	4,054	847	1,344	298

Albert Pujols' career postseason batting statistics

YEAR	TEAM	G	AB	R	H	2B
2001	St. Louis	5	18	1	2	0
2002	St. Louis	8	29	5	8	1
2004	St. Louis	15	58	15	24	4
2005	St. Louis	9	32	7	12	2
2006	St. Louis	4	15	3	5	1
Total		19	67	15	20	3

KEY:
G=Games
AB=At-Bats
R=Runs Scored
H=Hits
2B=Doubles
3B=Triples
HR=Home Runs
RBI=Runs Batted In
BB=Bases on Balls (Walks)
SO=Strikeouts
SB=Stolen Bases
CS=Caught Stealing
AVG.=Batting Average

3B	HR	RBI	BB	SO	SB	CS	AVG.
4	37	130	69	93	1	3	.329
2	34	127	72	69	2	4	.314
1	43	124	79	65	5	1	.359
2	46	123	84	52	5	5	.331
2	41	117	97	65	16	2	.330
1	49	137	92	50	7	2	.331
1	32	103	99	58	2	6	.327
13	282	861	592	452	38	23	.332

3B	HR	RBI	BB	SO	SB	CS	AVG.
0	1	2	2	2	0	0	.111
1	1	5	5	6	0	0	.276
0	6	14	8	6	0	0	.414
0	2	8	5	3	0	0	.375
0	1	3	1	4	0	0	.333
1	4	15	13	7	0	0	.299

CAREER ACHIEVEMENTS

- Won National League MVP in 2005

- Second all-time with 201 home runs in his first five seasons, trailing only Ralph Kiner's 215

- Seventh all-time with 621 RBIs in his first five seasons. Joe DiMaggio is first with 691 RBIs

- Fourth youngest player in history to reach 600 RBIs

- His 96 game-winning RBIs since 2001 leads the major leagues

- His 161 go-ahead RBIs since 2001 also leads the major leagues

- Fourth rookie in history to collect at least 30 home runs, 100 runs scored, and 100 RBIs while batting .300 or higher

- First player all time to collect at least 30 home runs, 100 runs scored, and 100 RBIs while batting .300 or higher in each of his first six seasons

- In 2003, won the Players Choice Award for the Major League Player of the Year and was named the National League's Outstanding Player. He also was chosen as the Major League Player of the Year by *The Sporting News*

- Named to the Arizona Fall League Hall of Fame

- Honored by New York with the 2005 Latino MVP Award

- Participated with the Dominican Republic team in the 2006 World Baseball Classic.

- Awarded the Gold Glove and earned the Marvin Miller Man of the Year Award from the MLB Players Association in 2006

CHAPTER NOTES

CHAPTER 1. A STAR IS DISCOVERED

1. Associated Press, "Pujols (14) sets homer record for April in victory," ESPN.com, April 29, 2006, <http://sports.espn.go.com/mlb/recap?gameId=260429124> (August 23, 2006).

2. Christopher Kirsch, "Thank you, Bobby Bonilla," March 17, 2006, <http://www.inwaltwetrust.com/?p=16> (August 24, 2006).

CHAPTER 2. A BOY AND HIS DREAMS

1. "Albert Pujols," jockbio.com, ongoing chronicle, <http://www.jockbio.com/Bios/Pujols/Pujols_mysay.html> (September 5, 2006).

2. Daniel G. Habib, "A Swing of Beauty," May 22, 2006, <http://sportsillustrated.cnn.com/2006/magazine/06/09/pujols0522/index.html> (September 4, 2006).

3. Larry Wigge, "On Another Level," *St. Louis Cardinals Gameday Magazine*, 2005, No. 4, pp. 34–43.

4. Ibid.

5. Ibid.

6. Ibid.

7. Daniel G. Habib, "A Swing of Beauty," May 22, 2006, <http://sportsillustrated.cnn.com/2006/magazine/06/09/pujols0522/index.html> (September 4, 2006).

8. Rick Dean, "Pujols could have been in a Kansas City uniform," *Topeka Capital-Journal* via Sports Radio 810 WHB, <http://www.810whb.com/scripts/archives/getStory.asp?article=12344> (September 3, 2006).

CHAPTER 3. BUILDING A RESUME

1. Rick Dean, "Pujols could have been in a Kansas City uniform," *Topeka Capital-Journal* via Sports Radio 810 WHB, <http://www.810whb.com/scripts/archives/getStory.asp?article=12344> (September 3, 2006).

2. Scott Lee, "Fry was 'all business' on field," *The Examiner's Sports Monthly*, January 16, 2004, <http://sportsmonthly.net/stories/011604/Spo_011604018.shtml> (August 29, 2006).

3. Sean Deveney, "Can't get no satisfaction," *The Sporting News*, May 18, 2006, <http://www.sportingnews.com/yourturn/viewtopic.php?t=93313> (September 1, 2006).

4. Randy Covitz, "Scout who signed Pujols looks back, now stocks shelves at Wal-Mart," *Kansas City Star*, May 23, 2006, <http://www.kansascity .com/mld/kansascity/sports/baseball/14646725.htm> (August 28, 2006).

5. Ibid.

6. Ibid.

7. Sean Deveney, "Can't get no satisfaction," *The Sporting News*, May 18, 2006, <http://www.sportingnews.com/yourturn/viewtopic.php?t=93313> (September 1, 2006).

CHAPTER 4. FALLING IN LOVE

1. "Christian Family Expo Special Guests," June 1, 2006, <http://www .christianfamilyexpo.com/guests.html> (August 23, 2006).

2. Ibid.

3. Tim Wendel, "Home Run Dads," *USA Weekend*, June 11, 2006, <http://www.usaweekend.com/06_issues/060611/060611baseballdads .html> (August 26, 2006).

4. "Christian Family Expo Special Guests," June 1, 2006, <http://www .christianfamilyexpo.com/guests.html> (August 23, 2006).

5. Kay Quinn, "Deidre Pujols Talks About Famous Husband, Faith, And Foundation To Help Others," ksdk.com, May 5, 2006, <http://www.ksdk.com /news/cover_story/cover_article.aspx?storyid=96299> (August 23, 2006).

6. Ibid.

7. Ibid.

8. Tim Wendel, "Home Run Dads," *USA Weekend*, June 11, 2006, <http://www.usaweekend.com/06_issues/060611/060611baseballdads .html> (August 26, 2006).

CHAPTER 5. WHO IS THAT ROOKIE?

1. *Baseball Almanac*, "Quotations From & About Albert Pujols," <http://www .baseball-almanac.com/quotes/albert_pujols_quotes.shtml> (September 1, 2006).

2. Ken Gurnik, "Schilling, Womack deliver D-Backs to NLCS," MLB.com, October 15, 2001, <http://mlb.mlb.com/NASApp/mlb/ws/news/ws_news _story_nl_2.jsp?article=10142001-2308> (September 1, 2006).

3. Larry Wigge, "On Another Level," *St. Louis Cardinals Gameday Magazine*, 2005, No. 4, pp. 34–43.

CHAPTER 6. PRACTICE MAKES PERFECT

1. *Baseball Almanac*, "Quotations From & About Albert Pujols," <http://www .baseball-almanac.com/quotes/albert_pujols_quotes.shtml> (September 1, 2006).

2. Ibid.

3. Ibid.

4. Daniel G. Habib, "A Swing of Beauty," May 22, 2006, <http://sportsillustrated.cnn.com/2006/magazine/06/09/pujols0522/index.html> (September 4, 2006).

5. *Baseball Almanac*, "Quotations From & About Albert Pujols," <http://www.baseball-almanac.com/quotes/albert_pujols_quotes.shtml> (September 1, 2006).

6. Daniel G. Habib, "A Swing of Beauty," May 22, 2006, <http://sportsillustrated.cnn.com/2006/magazine/06/09/pujols0522/index.html> (September 4, 2006).

7. *Baseball Almanac*, "Quotations From & About Albert Pujols," <http://www.baseball-almanac.com/quotes/albert_pujols_quotes.shtml> (September 1, 2006).

8. Bob Nightengale, "Big Mac retires on his terms," *USA TODAY Baseball Weekly*, November 21, 2001, <http://www.usatoday.com/sports/bbw/2001-11-14/2001-11-14-cover.htm> (September 3, 2006).

9. "'Worn out' McGwire retires from baseball," *ESPN.com news services*, November 13, 2001, <http://espn.go.com/mlb/news/2001/1111/1276851.html> (September 4, 2006).

10. Ibid.

CHAPTER 7. OVERCOMING JINXES AND MUCH MORE

1. Harvey Fialkov, "Cardinals' Albert Pujols shows no complacency in his play; National League Rookie of the Year in 2001 continues to produce as St. Louis' big gun in a powerful lineup - Sophomore Jinx? ... Never Heard of It," *Baseball Digest*, November 2002, <http://www.findarticles.com/p/articles/mi_m0FCI/is_11_61/ai_92521917> (September 4, 2006).

2. "Remembering Jack Buck," MLB.com, June 19, 2002, <http://mlb.mlb.com/NASApp/mlb/mlb/news/mlb_news.jsp?ymd=20020619&content_id=56848&vkey=news_mlb&fext=.jsp> (September 4, 2006).

3. Ibid.

4. "Cardinals' hurler Kile dead at 33," *Associated Press*, June 23, 2002, <http://espn.go.com/mlb/news/2002/0622/1397921.html> (September 4, 2006).

5. Ibid.

6. Paul C. Smith, "Cards lament missed chances," MLB.com, October 14, 2002, <http://mlb.mlb.com/NASApp/mlb/mlb/news/mlb_news.jsp?ymd=20021014&content_id=157490&vkey=cs2002news&fext=.jsp> (September 5, 2006).

7. Matthew Leach, "Morris valiant in loss to Giants," MLB.com, October 14, 2002, <http://mlb.mlb.com/NASApp/mlb/stl/news/stl_gameday_recap.jsp? ymd=20021014&content_id=158204&vkey=recap&fext=.jsp> (September 1, 2006).

8. Ibid.

9. Jack Etkin, "National League 2003 Batting Champion Albert Pujols: Cardinals slugger has performed at a high level of consistency in his first three major league seasons," *Baseball Digest*, February 2004, <http://www.findarticles .com/p/articles/mi_m0FCI/is_2_63/ai_112167125> (August 30, 2006).

CHAPTER 8. PUJOLS' DREAM: THE WORLD SERIES

1. Rich Draper, "Cards confident heading home," MLB.com, October 19, 2004, <http://mlb.mlb.com/NASApp/mlb/stl/news/stl_news.jsp?ymd=20041018& content_id=899564&vkey=news_stl&fext=.jsp> (August 28, 2006).

2. Matthew Leach, "Edmonds' homer evens up NLCS," MLB.com, October, 20, 2004, <http://mlb.mlb.com/NASApp/mlb/stl/news/stl_gameday_recap.jsp ?ymd=20041020&content_id=900869&vkey=recap&fext=.jsp> (August 27, 2006).

3. Matthew Leach, "Cards earn trip to World Series," MLB.com, October 21, 2004, <http://mlb.mlb.com/NASApp/mlb/stl/news/stl_gameday_recap.jsp? ymd=20041021&content_id=902331&vkey=recap&fext=.jsp> (August 26, 2006).

4. Mark Newman, "Fall Classic will be well red," MLB.com, October 22, 2004, <http://mlb.mlb.com/NASApp/mlb/stl/news/stl_news.jsp?ymd=20041022& content_id=902764&vkey=news_stl&fext=.jsp> (August 27, 2006).

5. Matthew Leach, "Cardinals shut out in clincher," MLB.com, October 27, 2004, <http://mlb.mlb.com/NASApp/mlb/stl/news/stl_gameday_recap.jsp? ymd=20041027&content_id=906939&vkey=recap&fext=.jsp> (August 26, 2006).

6. Ibid.

7. Larry Wigge, "On Another Level," *St. Louis Cardinals Gameday Magazine*, 2005, No. 4, pp. 34–43.

CHAPTER 9. BUILDING A FOUNDATION

1. "The Pujols Family Foundation is officially launched," Pujols Family Foundation, May 5, 2005, <http://www.pujolsfamilyfoundation.org/news 10.htm> (August 29, 2006).

2. Susan Fadem, "Swinging for the Fences — While her husband hits home runs for the Cardinals, Dee Dee Pujols dishes out some fantastic plays of her own," *St. Louis Woman Magazine*, April 2006, <http://www .stlouiswomanmag.com/covergallery/06/apr.html> (September 1, 2006).

3. Ibid.

4. Andrew Knox, "Albert Pujols: A Hero's Worship," CBN.com, <http://www .cbn.com/entertainment/sports/700club_albertpujols080206.aspx> (August 30, 2006).

5. Conor Nicholl, "Pujols raises money with Golf Classic," MLB.com, August 14, 2006, <http://mlb.mlb.com/NASApp/mlb/news/article.jsp?ymd= 20060814&content_id=1609594&vkey=news_stl&fext=.jsp&c_id=stl> (September 4, 2006).

6. Matthew Leach, "Notes: Golf Classic a success," MLB.com, July 9, 2004, <http://stlouis.cardinals.mlb.com/NASApp/mlb/stl/news/stl_news.jsp?ymd= 20040709&content_id=793964&vkey=news_stl&fext=.jsp> (September 1, 2006).

7. Nate Latsch, "Pujols family to start new foundation," MLB.com, May 5, 2005, <http://mlbplayers.mlb.com/NASApp/mlb/pa/news/article.jsp?ymd= 20050505&content_id=1039640&vkey=mlbpa_news&fext=.jsp> (August 23, 2006).

8. Sean Deveney, "Pujols thrives by never being satisfied," *The Sporting News*, May 19, 2006, <http://www.msnbc.msn.com/id/12862850/> (September 1, 2006).

9. Nate Latsch, "Pujols family to start new foundation," MLB.com, May 5, 2005, <http://mlbplayers.mlb.com/NASApp/mlb/pa/news/article.jsp?ymd =20050505&content_id=1039640&vkey=mlbpa_news&fext=.jsp> (August 23, 2006).

CHAPTER 10. AN MVP SEASON

1. Ken Gurnik, "Sanders sets NLDS RBI record," MLB.com, October 9, 2005, <http://mlb.mlb.com/NASApp/mlb/news/article.jsp?ymd–20051008& content_id=1243224&vkey=ps2005news&fext=.jsp> (September 5, 2006).

2. Matthew Leach, "Pujols keeps Cards' season alive," MLB.com, October 18, 2005, <http://mlb.mlb.com/NASApp/mlb/news/gameday_recap.jsp?ymd= 20051017&content_id=1253412&vkey=recap&fext=.jsp&c_id=stl> (September 5, 2006).

3. Ibid.

4. John Schlegel, "St. Louis savors memories of Busch," MLB.com, October 20, 2005, <http://mlb.mlb.com/NASApp/mlb/news/article_perspectives.jsp? ymd=20051019&content_id=1255124&vkey=perspectives&fext=.jsp> (September 3, 2006).

5. Matthew Leach, "Pujols earns first MVP Award," MLB.com, November 15, 2005, <http://stlouis.cardinals.mlb.com/NASApp/mlb/news/article.jsp?ymd =20051115&content_id=1268475&vkey=news_stl&fext=.jsp&c_id=stl> (September 1, 2006).

6. Matthew Leach, "Cards Secure 10th World Series title," MLB.com, October 28, 2006, <http://mlb.mlb.com/NASApp/mlb/news/gameday_recap.jsp? ymd=20061027&content_id=1725895&vkey=recap&fext=.jsp&c_id=stl> (November 13, 2006).

GLOSSARY

baseball scout—A person who watches college and high school players and reports about the players' skills to a Major League Baseball team.

batter's box—The four-foot by six-foot area that a batter must stand in when attempting to hit a pitch.

batting average—A baseball statistic arrived at by dividing a player's number of hits by his number of at-bats. Walks are not counted.

free agent—A player who may sign a contract with any team he chooses.

Gold Glove award—An award given to the top fielders at each position in each league.

infielder/outfielder—Position players. The outfield consists of a left fielder, center fielder, and right fielder. The infield consists of a first baseman, second baseman, shortstop, and third baseman.

Major League Baseball (MLB)—The highest professional level of baseball. It is comprised of two leagues, the American League and National League. There are thirty teams in Major League Baseball.

manager—The coach of a baseball team.

Minor League Baseball—Professional baseball leagues that operate at a level below Major League Baseball. The teams are affiliates of MLB teams.

MLB All-Star Game—A game held in the middle of the MLB season, pitting the best players from the National League against the best players from the American League. Also called the Midsummer Classic.

opposite-field hit—A hit that goes to the other side of the field than the side of the plate the batter is standing. A right-handed hitter would hit an opposite-field hit to right field.

pitching rotation—The game-by-game order in which a team starts its pitchers.

power hitter—A batter who is known for hitting extra-base hits.

RBIs— Runs batted in. The number of runs that score as a result of a batter getting a hit.

rookie—A player who is in his first season in the league.

series—A set number of games two teams will play against each other. The MLB playoffs are set in series. The first is the best-of-five divisional series. The second is the best-of-seven championship series, and the final is the best-of-seven World Series, also known as the Fall Classic.

slider—A pitch that is a combination of a curve ball and a fastball.

sophomore jinx—The myth that many players who do well in their rookie seasons will suffer slumps during their second years.

spring training—The practice period before the regular season during which MLB teams play exhibition games and determine which players will make their roster.

sweep—To win a series without the other team winning a single game.

Triple Crown—A feat accomplished by a batter who leads the league in the three major offensive categories—home runs, RBIs, and batting average.

walk-off home run—A home run that ends a game.

FOR MORE INFORMATION

FURTHER READING

Fischer, David. *Albert Pujols.* Chanhassen, Minn.: The Child's World, 2006.

Nemec, David, and Dave Zeman. *The Baseball Rookies Encyclopedia: The Most Authoritative Guide to Baseball's First-Year Players.* Dulles, Va.: Potomac Books, 2004.

Rains, Rob. *Albert the Great: The Albert Pujols Story.* Champaign, Ill.: Sports Publishing LLC, 2005.

WEB LINKS

Pujols Family Foundation:
http://www.pujolsfamilyfoundation.org

Pujols' page on stlouis.cardinals.mlb.com:
http://stlouis.cardinals.mlb.com/team/player.jsp?player_id=405395

Pujols' page on baseball-reference.com:
http://www.baseball-reference.com/p/pujolal01.shtml

Pujols' page on baseball-almanac.com:
http://www.baseball-almanac.com/players/player.php?p=pujolal01

INDEX

D

E

F

G

H

I